HOW TO SPOT A TERRORIST

BEFORE IT'S TOO LATE!

For information about this title or to order other books and/or electronic media, contact the publisher:
SafeLife Publishing, LLC
5320 N. 16th Street
Suite 202
Phoenix, AZ 85016
www. SafeLifePublishing.com
info@safelifepublishing.com

ISBNs: 978-0-9976015-0-3 (Print)
       978-0-9976015-1-0 (eBook)

Printed in the United States of America

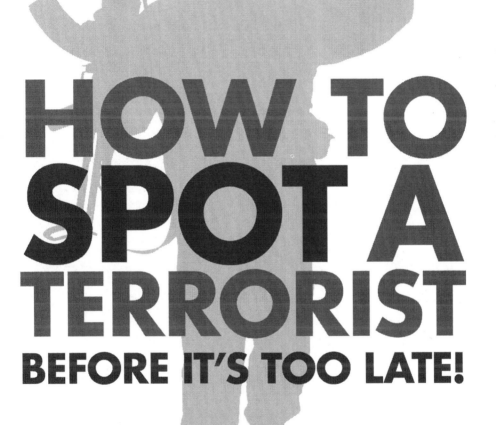

HOW TO SPOT A TERRORIST

BEFORE IT'S TOO LATE!

John G. Iannarelli

FBI SPECIAL AGENT (RET.)

SafeLife™
PUBLISHING

LEGAL DISCLAIMER

The information in this book has been prepared to assist you with learning ways to protect yourself and your family by recognizing potential threats of violence, to include the threat of terrorism. It is meant to be used as a helpful guide, but should not be considered as a complete resource on this subject. The purchaser and/or reader of this book should seek the advice of appropriate professionals for more in-depth instruction on the subjects presented.

The author and publisher have made every effort to ensure the accuracy of the information within this book was correct at time of publication. The author/publisher does not assume and hereby disclaims any liability to any party for any loss, damage, or disruption caused by errors or omissions, whether such errors or omissions result from accident, negligence, or any other cause. The information contained within this book is strictly for educational purposes. If you wish to apply ideas contained in this book, you are taking full responsibility for your actions. Any person or entity that relies on information obtained from this book does so at his or her own risk

The author and publisher, to the fullest extent permitted by law, disclaims all warranties, either expressed or implied, statutory or otherwise, including but not limited to any implied warranties.

DEDICATION

For my daughter Samantha and my son Garrett. I am sorry for all those times that duty called me away and I could not be with you. I missed birthdays, holidays, graduations, and a host of other events while you were growing up, but I always did so with the purpose of trying to help create a world in which to keep you safe. I wish I had been home more and thank you for always forgiving my absence. I love you more than you can ever know.

I also wish to acknowledge the victims of terrorism and their families. You have given more than anyone to this cause and have motivated me to write this book in order to help protect others. Rest assured there are many professionals out there who dedicate their very existence to this ongoing battle every day. Your sacrifices will never have been in vain.

MADRID • JERUSALEM
WASHINGTON • LOCKERBIE
CHARLESTON • MADRID
ISTANBUL • WASHINGTON
MUMBAI • TUCSON
OKLAHOMA CITY • LONDON
SHANKSVILLE • SOUSSE
LOS ANGELES • JAKATA
SAN BERNARDINO • MOSCOW
PARIS • CHARLESTON
FORT HOOD • ISTANBUL

CONTENTS

ACKNOWLEDGEMENTS

This book could not have been written without the assistance and efforts of others, for whom I owe a debt of gratitude.

First and foremost, I would like to thank Gregg Ostro, president of Go Media Companies in Phoenix. It was Gregg who came up with the idea for this book, and he encouraged (pushed) me to write it. Gregg also took on various projects in support of the book, which included going through the book line by line to ensure the message was properly delivered. Additionally, Gregg sparked the media's interest even before the book was complete, enabling the word to get out that there are ways the average person can contribute not only to combating terrorism, but also to keeping themselves and their families safe in the process. Without Gregg there would not be a book and you the reader would not know "How to stop a terrorist before it is too late!"

Gregg has two fine employees among his staff: Ben Ostro and Jade Bunda, both of whom I must thank for offering their near daily assistance to the project.

Robby Ward did a tremendous job contributing to the editing process, weeding out the unnecessarily repetitive words and helping me focus on the important narrative. I am sure if I had provided Robby with this page of acknowledgements, his ability to remove unnecessary verbiage would have resulted in you already having finished reading this section.

Bill Greaves of Concept West Graphic Design is a gifted artist who took the idea for the book and singlehandedly designed the book's cover, creating an image that truly captured the message.

Michele DeFilippo and Ronda Rawlins of 1106 Design was wonderful to work with, using their talents to ensure the manuscript was edited, typeset, and all the other magic that is done to transfer words from an electronic file into printed pages in a book, as well as transferring them back into an electronic file for Kindle readers.

Finally, I would be remiss not to offer sincere thanks to all of the members of our military and law enforcement communities, both within the United States and aboard, who work so tirelessly to keep us safe. It is solely because of your efforts that we are able to feel safe in our homes and live the lives that we wish. Your jobs are never ending, tremendously stressful and, unfortunately, sometimes thankless. Rest assured that you have many supporters who appreciate what you do; thank God for altruistic persons such as yourselves. You have my continued respect and admiration. I hope that in some way this book will make your jobs a little easier and keep you, along with the rest of us, safer.

PREFACE

I have written *How to Spot a Terrorist* with the expressed intent of giving the public a form of empowerment. So frequently we hear the news of some danger, violence, or attack, and many of us come away from this information with nothing more than fear. So little on the subject of terrorism is shared in the way of practical knowledge. I thought it would be a good idea to take a few simple concepts, which are well known throughout the law enforcement community, and share these insights with the average citizen. Rather than feeling helpless and fearful, such information can instill a bit of reassurance, as well as create the ability to protect our homeland should such an occasion arise.

In case anyone might think that I am giving away secrets to the terrorists, you can be assured that everything within this book is derived from public sources. All of the information has been available to the public for some time. Just as importantly, the terrorists are aware that law enforcement knows the things that a terrorist will do. And yet, the terrorists are undeterred in their desire to attack us. Law enforcement's knowledge of their actions does not discourage the terrorists. So, nothing within this book will give a terrorist an advantage. However, the knowledge you will gain could very well put a terrorist at a distinct disadvantage.

As you will see from reading this book, there are a number of things that cannot be changed if a terrorist wants to carry out an attack. They will still do certain things in certain ways. What will change is that by learning of what to be aware, you might be able to spot a terrorist and potentially stop an attack before it's too late.

INTRODUCTION

"The world will not be destroyed by those who do evil, but by those who watch them without doing anything."

—Albert Einstein*

Today, we as Americans need to both recognize and accept the threats that exist around us, as we now live in a world with local-to-global terror. I've written this book to guide you to fulfill Einstein's lifesaving wisdom (see epigraph above) by helping to educate you and your loved ones on *How to Spot a Terrorist—Before It's Too Late!* It's easy to understand and focuses on ten things we can all do to help prevent terrorism, including what to do if terror finds you or your loved ones.

If you are going to learn how to spot terror, you need to know how to profile terrorists' actions. Yes, *profile;* it's not a dirty word. I am not talking about someone's race, ethnicity, or religion. I'm talking about recognizing the behaviors and actions of terrorists and their helpers as they get in position to attack. In law enforcement terminology these are known as "indicators," and that's my definition of profiling, which is a key component of what you'll learn in this book.

All of us need to be able to recognize the telltale actions that fit the profile of those who plot terror against us. You need to know how to recognize behaviors and actions that are often obvious, unusual, odd, unsettling, or suspicious activities and know how to safely notify law enforcement of your observations and concerns.

---

*Albert Einstein, considered one of the most brilliant minds of the 20th century, was a Jewish German-born theoretical physicist who emigrated to the United States to escape the terror of Nazism. He developed the general theory of relativity, E=mc².

If more Americans knew how to spot terror activity, maybe some, if not all, of the lethal and devastating attacks in our homeland that occurred during my tenure as an FBI Special Agent could have been prevented.

In February 1993, terrorists hit the United States by parking a truck with a bomb in the basement of one of the World Trade Center towers in New York City. This event was a game changer for law enforcement and all of us in the United States. Terrorists had brought death, destruction, and disaster directly to American soil.

The bombing suspects were quickly arrested when they returned to the vehicle rental agency to claim their deposit. By that time the FBI had already identified the vehicle that was used in the attack and were waiting at the rental agency on the off chance these criminals would be foolish enough to return.

A few years later, America experienced an act of domestic terrorism on an unprecedented scale when Timothy McVeigh, a disgruntled former Army soldier who blamed others for his own failures and shortcomings, decided to attack the US government by bombing the Alfred P. Murrah Federal Building in Oklahoma City. On April 19, 1995, at 9:02 a.m., a Ryder truck that McVeigh and others had packed with explosive materials destroyed the entire front of the nine-story Murrah building and ripped it apart, killing 168 people, including nineteen little children who were in the building's day care center.

McVeigh made his getaway in a car he had parked nearby, but a sharp-eyed Oklahoma State Trooper stopped him, noticing an improper license plate on his getaway vehicle. When McVeigh was discovered to be wearing a concealed weapon that he did not have a license to carry, the trooper took him into custody. It was while McVeigh sat in jail awaiting his court hearing regarding the weapon he was carrying that the FBI once again was able to identify the vehicle used in the attack. After tracing the vehicle to the rental agency, they were provided a name that led them to McVeigh. It should be noted that he did not use his real name when he rented the Ryder truck, nor did he give his proper name to law enforcement when he was later arrested. Nevertheless, just a few pieces of information proved to be enough to connect McVeigh to the crime and for the FBI to apprehend him before he was released from jail.

On September 11, 2001, terrorism on US soil reared its ugly head in an attack on an unparalleled scale. Terrorists commandeered four US airplanes in mid-flight and used them as missiles to attack locations in New York City and Washington, DC. All but one of the four hijacked planes fulfilled their objectives. The fourth plane was thought to be headed for the US Capitol. It was a moment we should all be proud of as passengers on this doomed flight fought back against the attackers. As a result of their heroism, the plane went down in a field in Shanksville, Pennsylvania, instead of striking its intended target.

Combined with the other three planes that fulfilled their terrorist objectives, three thousand citizens lost their lives that tragic day, along with thousands more injured and billions of dollars in damage. It brought America to a near standstill. The physical recovery took years to complete, and in some cases is still ongoing. The emotional recovery continues and will probably never be truly completed. And the memory of that day changed the way Americans view their safety forever.

Even though the events of 9/11 changed the way most of us view the world, little has changed what really impacts the average citizen's day-to-day lives. Though most of us don't like standing in longer lines at the airport, we do it so that authorities can identify potential terror suspects before they can hurt us. Other than this and a few other tangible changes to our lives, such as passing through metal detectors and carrying clear bags into stadiums, life has mostly remained the same for the moment.

We continue to go about our lives knowing that danger exists, but we rarely think that danger is going to affect us personally. We must change our thinking. Terrorists are increasing their efforts to hit us in the homeland; therefore, we need to be on the lookout for potential terror indicators. If we spot them, we need to notify law enforcement.

The two major attacks in Paris during 2015, and the recent attack in San Bernardino, California, are harsh reminders that the world of the terrorist threats remains very real. They still want to carry out their message through fear. They still want to impose their way of life upon others. They still want to do us harm.

Ask yourself, while you may wish to believe the chances of you or a loved one actually ever being a victim of terrorism is statistically remote, do you feel safe? As good as the FBI and others may be at protecting us by preventing events that we will probably never hear about or realize how close we may have come, do you feel helpless about the fact that you might be in the wrong place at the wrong time? Do you wish you could protect yourself and your loved ones, rather than just hoping others can successfully do it for you? Fortunately, there are ways that all of us can assist in battling terrorism.

This book outlines simple and basic steps that are easy and that all of us can do to help keep our family, our community, and ourselves safe. Knowing what to look for, to whom you should report what you see, and what to do should something occur, changes you from being a victim to a proactive defender of your own well-being.

Knowledge is power, and in the following pages you will find simple suggestions to guide you on how to spot terror indicators and help law enforcement by reporting what you see. To help you do this, I've built into this book what I call The Iannarelli Terrorist Indicator Profile, or I-TIP for short.

In each chapter I will provide you with specific I-TIPs to help you identify potential terrorist planning activities. Use these tips to spot terror and let authorities know . . . before it is too late!

CHAPTER ONE

SUPPLIES

Terrorists Need Things;
We Need to Spot and Report Unusual Purchases

"But there's one thing we must all be clear about: terrorism is not the pursuit of legitimate goals by some sort of illegitimate means. Whatever the murderers may be trying to achieve, creating a better world certainly isn't one of their goals. Instead, they are out to murder innocent people."

—Salman Rushdie*

It was a domestic terror disaster that sadly ended in an inferno of flames and gunfire including the death of innocents, brave first responders, and the complete destruction of a building complex. Generally, this deadly event is known as the Standoff at the Branch Dravidian Compound in Waco, Texas. It was a violent episode that serves as a clear and powerful example of the terrorists' need for supplies. It also illustrates how more aware and educated Americans, learning how to spot and report unusual supply collection, could prevent a horrendous loss of life.

David Koresh, the self-anointed leader of the Branch Davidian Church, and his fellow homegrown terrorists had been accumulating large amounts of firepower. According to affidavits filed in support of the original search warrant requested by the Federal Bureau of

---

*Salman Rushdie is a British Indian writer. His novel, *The Satanic Verses* (New York: Random House, 1988), was the center of a major controversy that provoked protests from Muslims in several countries. This culminated in a 1989 fatwa by Ayatollah Khomeini, who was the supreme leader of Iran at the time, calling for his assassination. Rushdie remains under protection.

Alcohol, Tobacco, Firearms, and Explosives (ATF), information had been obtained from various witnesses that the Davidian compound was receiving a large assortment of weapons and ammunition. This aroused the ATF's suspicion as to why a religious organization was collecting such things. The subsequent events, including the shooting of twenty ATF agents by Branch Dravidian personnel, showed that they were not who they pretended to be.

The information provided to the ATF about the guns and ammunition purchases came from some of the businesses that sold the weapons. Essentially, those who were in the very business of selling these items were able to recognize that something was amiss and alerted law enforcement. This is just one example of how acquiring supplies can be an indicator that potential terrorists may be at work and what we can do to spot such indicators of terror.

At Waco, the attempted raid by special agents of the ATF ended with four agents killed and sixteen others injured. After more than fifty days of negotiation with David Koresh and his followers, and the fact that conditions were deteriorating inside of the compound for the children of church members who were being held there with no option to leave, the government eventually decided to make entry. The Davidians, dedicated followers of Koresh, elected to end matters on their own terms and set fire to the compound, killing almost everyone who chose to remain inside. Only the selfless acts of FBI Hostage Rescue Team Operators, who risked their own lives in the line of fire, were able to save several of the Davidians, who even then were reluctant to be rescued.

Let's look back to look ahead. A church that is buying thousands of bullets and volumes of other potential death-inflicting materials: that is how all of this began. They needed supplies. We need to recognize unusual needs such as this as early as possible in order to report to law enforcement.

Purchasing or, in particular, stealing items—such as explosives, weapons, ammunition, or anything that can be used to make a bomb—is a good indicator that someone is engaging in further criminal activities, and there is a strong possibility that they also have a terroristic intent. Not everything is as obvious as guns and ammo.

Large qualities of fertilizer can be used to make explosives, which was one of the indicators in the Oklahoma City bombing. Timothy McVeigh, who was eventually convicted and executed for his horrendous crime, along with the help of a few others, purchased 55-gallon drums, along with ammonium nitrate and fertilizer in a large enough quantity to fill their rented truck.

This explosive mix was enough to bring down an entire building and even melted and twisted steel. Concrete and stone became mere rubble. Families lost their loved ones, and injuries sustained will impact entire lifetimes. Watchful eyes and reporting might have prevented the attack.

Who would think that beauty supplies could be deadly? The chemicals found in many over-the-counter beauty supplies, in sufficient quantity, can be an explosive mix.

I'm convinced lives were saved in Denver when, in 2009, a terrorist attempted to explain to the beauty supply stores he shopped at that he had many girlfriends, hence the need for so many supplies. Fortunately, in that case, store operators spotted the unusual purchases and alerted authorities, which enabled law enforcement prevention.

Fireworks are commonly for sale these days, especially during some holiday seasons throughout the year. We can be safer by noticing excessive purchases or suspicious questions about the power of the fireworks. As an example, the Boston Marathon bombers purchased large amounts of fireworks and used the gunpowder within them to make their bombs.

Any extremist or "lone wolf,"—someone not acting on the direction of another person but, rather, acting on his or her own—could repackage the explosives in fireworks as an improvised explosive device, also known as an IED. There can be a fine line between purchasing materials for ordinary use and stockpiling dangerous or suspicious items. If you see someone behaving strangely at your neighborhood fireworks stand—asking questions that suggest some other use beyond casual entertainment—it might be a good time to say something to police. If it seems odd enough, let law enforcement know and they'll determine the appropriate action, if any.

Uniform stores should also be vigilant by looking for those seeking to acquire military or police uniforms that may not necessarily have the proper reason to buy them.

In addition to uniforms, store owners should watch for purchases that could be used to help someone impersonate an official, such as military or police decals that can be placed on vehicles, or equipment for making official-looking access badges or police badges, which can then help them facilitate entry into restricted locations.

All of these items have lawful and proper purposes, but only when they are permitted to be in the right hands. Those who market these items should ensure that the purchasers have the right to do so and, when in doubt, should listen to their intuition if something does not seem right.

Another thing to spot is the unusual purchase of electronic circuit boards. Bomb making has become more sophisticated, and the use of electronic circuitry is common in the design of explosives, which can be set off remotely via a cell phone or an electronic timer.

Of course, many people in the computer and electronics field purchase these items every day, but those in the sales industry have a good understanding of what these items are used for. If the purchaser does not seem to have the understanding of or expertise for proper purposes for these materials, a call to local authorities might be the best course of action.

These are just a few of the items that are available every day from numerous retailers that have a legitimate use, but when put in the hands of those who wish to do us harm, they can also be utilized to manufacture terror.

Maintaining a healthy degree of skepticism, including being sure what you see "adds up" and contacting the authorities if something doesn't seem right, can help us prevent disaster before it's too late.

I-TIP: Terrorists Need Things. We Need to Spot and Report Unusual Purchases.

CHAPTER TWO

SURVEILLANCE

They're watching, testing, and plotting.
We must spot, watch, and report.

"There is no doubt that our nation's security and defeating terrorism trump all other priorities."

—Arlen Specter*

McVeigh went through the building filled with workers, scouting and planning before his truck of explosives blew up and killed 168 people and injured nearly seven hundred other innocent Americans. He was conducting surveillance at the building, observing security procedures and law enforcement presence, as well as deciding how best to carry out his plans while still being able to get away. If only someone had known how to spot McVeigh during his terror-driven surveillance, maybe his plan of death and destruction might have been discovered, reported to authorities, and stopped before it was too late.

The homegrown terrorist and coward that destroyed the Alfred P. Murrah building didn't just randomly target this building. He was methodical in selecting his location for the attack. After choosing his location, he took the time to walk the hallways and make note of which federal agencies were located inside.

---

*Arlen Specter is a Former US Senator (Pennsylvania) and chairman of the Senate Select Committee on Intelligence.

McVeigh knew that ATF and Secret Service agents worked in the building and could be targeted. He also knew there was a child care center and that he would be killing young children of the federal employees. Prior to his attack McVeigh conducted surveillance.

Surveillance is the attentive observation of a person or place for the purpose of obtaining information. Often a terrorist will gather information about a potential target during the planning stages of an attack in an effort to identify potential security weaknesses that might be targeted.

Surveillance does not have to be just watching a building. A terrorist can observe security personnel as they come and go, count the number of security guards that are on duty at any given time, learn their routines of patrol, watch when they take breaks, or if they are absent for long periods of time.

For our part, as average citizens, we must begin to look for those who are conducting surveillance for terror purposes. We need to watch for those who seem unusual in their looking and poking around to gather information.

A terrorist's surveillance can also include testing security to see how thorough they are, possibly by trying to drive a vehicle into a secure area with items that would be considered contraband if the vehicle were to be searched. Such use of surveillance could reveal an opportunity for the terrorist to plant a car bomb.

The terrorist attack at the World Trade Center in 1993 included a plan that had surveillance as a key element. The terrorists who perpetrated this attack checked out the parking garage of the North Tower, where they eventually decided to park a truck bomb containing 1,336 pounds of urea nitrate–hydrogen that was detonated. The terrorists had hoped that the North Tower would topple and crash into the South Tower, causing both towers to fall and kill thousands of innocent people. Although the towers did not topple and the terrorists plan ultimately failed, their efforts resulted in six people being killed and more than a thousand others injured.

A terrorist's surveillance can also be in the form of testing security by walking into restricted areas to determine if they will be challenged. This follows the thought process that if you look like you belong, no one will question you. Terrorists might simply act as if they know where they are going as they walk through a building, all the while conducting surveillance, including gathering intelligence on what they see.

Terrorists will use familiarity tactics to get in and see the target and make plans. In 2007, six would-be terrorists plotted to attack the Army base at Fort Dix, New Jersey. As part of their preparation, several of the terrorists posed as pizza delivery drivers so they could drive onto the base and check out the buildings and routes. Along the way, military security became accustomed to seeing them enter the property to make deliveries, which naturally lessened security's suspicions of the "delivery" persons. Fortunately, their plot was discovered and the terrorists were arrested by the FBI before they were able to carry out an attack. (By the way, the terrorists posing as pizza delivery drivers is also known as *impersonation*, which I cover in the next chapter).

Likewise, probing or testing the perimeter of a fence, facility, or its security systems is a logical course of surveillance action for a terrorist to take in the planning stages, but can also be a sign that we can spot and report to law enforcement.

Some of the indicators that a person is conducting surveillance include taking photographs of locations that might not normally be noteworthy. It is one thing to take photos of a tourist destination, but what about taking photos of a power plant, a bridge, a military installation, or even a shopping mall? We need to be watching.

Any one of these situations might be absolutely innocent, but as has been mentioned previously, if something seems out of the ordinary it pays to let the authorities know. They will decide what actions should be taken, if any.

Keep your eyes open for the use of modern technologies. A terrorist may not be as conspicuous as using a camera. Just like everyone else today terrorists are carrying cell phones with built-in digital cameras, along with other technologies that can take photographs and video discreetly, enabling them to blend in without being seen. Be ready to spot and report what looks suspicious.

Just as a terrorist conducting surveillance might be seen taking photographs, they could also be seen taking notes, drawing diagrams, making notations on maps, or studying their potential targets from a distance with binoculars. Again, it may all be perfectly innocent, but then again it might not. If you feel that what you spot is suspicious, and you think someone might be engaging in surveillance for a criminal purpose, let the police know.

The lesson here is that most attacks involve some form of surveillance. It might be as innocent in appearance as loitering for a period of time in a particular place to watch persons come and go, or it can be as sophisticated as studying the timing of traffic lights and commuter patterns. However, now you know that if you see someone hanging out or behaving in a suspicious way, such as checking out an employee-only entrance at a shopping mall, or examining the integrity of a fence alongside of an airport, or taking pictures of something not otherwise deemed noteworthy by the general public, they may be conducting surveillance for nefarious purposes. Advise the police that you saw something that looks strange. Law enforcement receives inquiries like that all the time, and as long as the call is genuine, in this post-9/11 world, they are more than willing to check it out.

I-TIP: They're watching, testing, and plotting. We must spot, observe, and report.

CHAPTER THREE

IMPERSONATION

They pretend. We defend by spotting, reporting the imposters.

"Nobody made a greater mistake than he who did nothing because he could only do a little."

—Sir Edmund Burke*

Police worried about terrorists impersonating security personnel during Pope Francis's visit to the United States in 2015. National Guardsmen in Illinois might have been gunned down or injured because of terror trickery. Is that really a cop or medical responder? What about that guy with a media pass and big TV camera: legitimate or not?

It's sad to say, but if we are going to do our best to stop terrorists before it's too late, we need to think it could be Halloween any day, 24/7. It's called *impersonation,* and it's the art and science of pretending to be someone else and fooling others. Terrorists engaging in impersonation can be a deceptive tool of violence and death that, with your awareness and reporting, can and must be taken away from would-be attackers.

Welcome to the world of amazing technology where we have access in stores and online to just about everything we need to look as if we were a doctor, public works technician, law enforcement official, or

---

*Sir Edmund Burke is an historic Irish author, orator, philosopher, and member of Parliament remembered for his support of the American Revolution.

even an elderly person seemingly wheelchair bound. Terrorists know this, and we need to understand it as well.

During the Pope's Fall 2015 visit to the United States, American law enforcement was concerned about the possibility of terrorists trying to launch an attack by impersonating first responders like police, firefighters, and emergency medical technicians (EMTs). By impersonating first responders terrorists could potentially use uniforms and false identification to enter secure areas, wreak their havoc, and then slip away undetected while the real authorities are responding to the scene.

The main goal of a terrorist who utilizes impersonation is to further their attack plan and do harm to unsuspecting citizens, as well as attacking brave first responders.

In March 2015, twenty-two-year-old Army National Guard soldier Hasan Edmonds hatched a plan to kill dozens at a US military installation in Illinois. He provided his uniforms to one of his cousins, who was also attempting to recruit others into the plot. The cousin and his accomplices, using Edmonds uniforms, were going to slip onto the base (where Edmonds had trained) and shoot unarmed military personnel. Fortunately, the FBI got wind of the plan and Edmonds was arrested as he attempted to board a flight in Chicago bound for the Middle East, where he intended to use his military training to fight on behalf of the Islamic State in Iraq and Syria (ISIS).*

While you should be on the lookout for these acts in America, if you travel abroad be aware that these tactics have been commonly used elsewhere around the world.

Before the 2015 terrorist attacks in Paris, French authorities arrested ISIS sympathizer Sid Ahmed Ghlam, a twenty-four-year-old Algerian

---

*ISIS is a radical political Sunni Muslim organization whose aim is to establish an Islamic state in the Middle East region. Their proposed territorial boundaries include Syria, Lebanon, Israel, Jordan, the Palestinian territories, and southeastern Turkey.

national, and foiled his alleged plot to attack a church in Southern France. In addition to weapons, bulletproof vests, and notes detailing possible targets, Ghlam was also in possession of police armbands, which French authorities believed he was going to use to facilitate the attack by impersonating law enforcement.

This potential threat of impersonation is difficult to defend against; in the United States there are many businesses that sell uniform and equipment to all first responders, and little is required by way of verification to make such purchases. A terrorist can easily produce an official-looking but fake ID card identifying himself or herself as a police officer. That would enable him or her to purchase all sorts of uniforms and supplies without arousing suspicion (unless the salesperson had a keen eye and spotted that it wasn't official). However, these purchases are often even easier for the would-be terrorists, who are shopping via the Internet, and can obtain clothing, weapons, and tactical gear with minimal confirmation required of their employment status.

So, how do we spot these impersonating sources of terror? Even if terrorists obtain uniforms and equipment, they still might not perfectly fit in. Be on the lookout for imposters through indicators such as uniforms that don't appear to fit properly, or perhaps the person wearing it is sloppy in their appearance, or if the uniform is incomplete (perhaps it has a missing nametag). Likewise, are they driving emergency vehicles that appear overloaded with personnel? Most law enforcement personnel won't sit in the back of a police car because the back seat is designed for prisoners, as the doors can only be opened from the outside. Also, criminals tend to be pretty filthy, and cops know better than to sit where criminals have been.

While much of the focus of this chapter has been on impersonation of first responders, terrorists can become other "characters" to achieve their goals. Terrorists might impersonate a mail carrier or other delivery person in order to easily enter a building and make inquires to target their terrorist attacks.

Likewise, posing as a reporter or member of the media would give a terrorist access to locations beyond that of the average citizen, also enabling them to ask probing questions. In one such case, a terrorist attacker pretending to be a foreign journalist was able to get close enough to an Israeli soldier to stab him. As the solider tried to flee, the imposter chased after him with a knife, but was fortunately shot and killed by other military personnel who were present before the attacker could inflict further injury.

Watch out for people who seem out of place and may be present under false pretenses, as they could have a dangerous hidden motive. The impersonation of law enforcement, military, or even company personnel doesn't just happen in films like *Mission Impossible*. Terrorists are assuming roles in real life to hurt us. This is why you and I must use our ability to spot the unusual and the seemingly fake or "just not right," and then report the impersonator.

It goes without saying that people trying to impersonate and pass themselves off as someone they're not should be considered suspicious and a potential danger. If you see someone who seems suspiciously out of place, wearing attire that seems off, or pretending to be someone that they're not, notify the *real* police immediately!

I-TIP: They pretend. We defend by spotting and reporting those who impersonate.

CHAPTER FOUR

SOCIAL MEDIA

Terrorists use social media to plan, recruit, lie, trick, and kill. We must spot their posts and report to law enforcement.

"Cyber terrorism could also become more attractive as the real and virtual worlds become more closely coupled . . . to the Internet."

—*Dorothy Denning**

During the investigation of the bloody Boston Marathon bombings, law enforcement officials learned that friends and acquaintances reportedly spotted social media posts and more by the diabolical Tsarnaev brothers. Unfortunately, no one reported it before it was too late. ISIS and other terror groups, both small and large, are using social media to plan how to bomb, kill, and injure us.

Dzhokhar Tsarnaev, the only survivor of the two individuals responsible for the Boston Marathon bombings, admitted to investigators that he and his brother were homegrown terrorists, radicalized solely online, and were not directly connected to any terrorist groups. Just as importantly, they learned to construct their bombs from an online al-Qaeda terrorism magazine.

Yet, the Tsarnaev brothers' online activities also provided opportunities for them to be stopped by those who came in contact with them through social media.

---

*Dorothy Denning is a former professor of computer science and director of the Georgetown Institute of Information Assurance.

Friends of the Tsarnaev brothers reportedly were aware of their interests in radical sites. Likewise, many read postings by the Tsarnaev brothers that were sympathetic to terrorist causes. If just one person who was aware of these online activities had come forward and privately notified law enforcement officials, the Tsarnaev brothers' deadly attack might have been prevented.

The FBI says Islamic radicals are using social media to communicate and that it needs better access to these communications. However, the private sector remains hesitant to work with government agencies, citing concerns about privacy. Within law enforcement communities the lack of access to these communications is referred to as the "Going Dark" problem, and as the debate continues over how a balance between improved access and privacy rights can be achieved, the terrorists continue their online activities. But, perhaps right now you can do what the government cannot.

Facebook, YouTube, Instagram, Twitter, and countless other social media sites are sources of communication for the twenty-first century. It is a great way to socialize, share information, and help shape identities. Meanwhile, the Internet has never been exactly safe for unsuspecting victims, as thieves, pedophiles, and other deviants also use it daily, trying to rip us off or get their sick desires fulfilled. Now the Internet can be even more dangerous than ever with deadly terrorists online.

While you and your loved ones are happily and innocently engaging with friends and others through social media, deadly terror agents are using the power of the Internet to communicate plans, recruit members, and plot our death and destruction. As Americans, when using the Internet, we need to be aware to spot terror's use of social media and let law enforcement officials know right away if we suspect something.

Osama bin Laden was notorious for sending his audio and video recordings directly to the Arabic television network Al-Jazeera, who was all too happy to report his messages of hate.

Another great advantage terrorists have by using social media is that they are not engaging in one-way communications. Social media platforms like Twitter enable a dialog. Terrorists can post their messages of hate and engage their followers in debate, cleverly persuading others to their terrorist way of thinking by distorting the true facts, and, in doing so, winning over more converts.

ISIS and other terrorist groups are actively engaged in all forms of social media to recruit for this cause. Terrorist organizations have mastered the use of social media and are more effective than many legitimate businesses in attracting followers and selling their products. Unfortunately, what terrorists are selling is violence and death. Furthermore, even if every police officer in the country was monitoring the Internet all the time, there would still be more posts by terrorists than law enforcement officials could handle. That's why the law enforcement community needs all of us to help by being their eyes and ears.

Many people throughout the United States and the rest of the world, especially those who are young and feeling lonely or disconnected, are searching for a sense of identity. These people can be vulnerable and unsuspecting. Terrorists recognize the strong human desire to belong and prey upon their potential terror team members by offering them a chance to belong, while providing a purpose and mission in their lives. It's how gangs are commonly formed, as they often recruit members by making the lonely and unsuspecting feel like they matter—like they're family.

Here's what you need to know to help protect yourself, those in your life circle, and our fellow Americans. Terrorist organizations rely on social media because it is not only cheap and accessible, but it is a way they can share their messages with the public masses without concern of being edited and filtered by the regular mass media outlets. Through the use of social media, terrorists have complete control of what they say and what others will hear, see, and read.

Terrorists do this to recruit members to join up and fight for the cause, whether it is traveling overseas to distant lands or launching terrorist-inspired attacks right here at home. Additionally, women are often recruited to be married off to the male terrorists, but in some cases they are put to work doing the actual fighting. Such offers to fight for a "cause" might even seem glamorous to some women, presented with the opportunity to leave home and participate, or support their "brave" fighter terrorist husband. However, such glamorous visions are often terminal. Just look at the case of two teenage women who married ISIS fighters.

In November 2015, it was reported that one young lady, a seventeen-year-old, and her friend left their home in Austria to join ISIS. They were then married to ISIS fighters and sent off to be with their new husbands near the battlefield. After one of these misguided girls was killed in a battle, the other decided she no longer wanted to take part and attempted to leave the group. As punishment for her "crime" of trying to leave, she was beaten to death. A teen beaten to death by terrorist men simply because she had changed her mind.

Terrorist organizations use social media not just for recruiting, but also to incite fear. Most terrorist groups have websites where they will post information and make threats. All too common are the graphic videos of brutal beheadings that ISIS has posted online, available to be viewed by anyone and posted to be a warning to those who don't give in to their demands.

Many ask why the government doesn't take down these terror websites. The reality is that most of these websites are hosted by companies located overseas, over which the United States has no authority. Likewise, in some cases the more benign websites may be spreading propaganda, but are not breaking any laws. This means that these individuals enjoy the protection of the First Amendment Freedom of Speech that, ironically, is one of the very fundamental rights they seek to destroy.

Terror websites and postings can be a tool for law enforcement and all of us to spot the plans and activities of terrorists. Should you come across such sites, read what is being said, and try to determine whom they are attempting to recruit and what possible threats they are making. If you have the ability to determine who is hosting the websites, bring it to the attention of the web providers. In many cases it is difficult, if not impossible, for these companies to self-police. The web hosting company probably doesn't even know what is happening and will appreciate being notified. Obviously, hosting a terrorist's website, especially if it is a US-based company, is bad for business. This is where you can be an asset, before it's too late.

If a website is spewing dangerous messages, also be sure to first bring it to the attention of law enforcement officials so that they are aware. The authorities might wish to work with the web provider in an effort to determine who is posting the information in question.

And for anyone reading this who may have concerns that am I suggesting we censor free speech, allow me to state that I am absolutely not! The US Supreme Court has ruled that providing "material support" to a terrorist organization is in itself a crime. The distinction is that posting terrorist beliefs on the Internet might be considered freedom of speech, but actively posting Internet messages that seek to recruit others to commit terrorist acts would be considered "material support" and, hence, a violation of the law.

Finally, here is one last way that social media can be used to actually thwart the terrorists. Although I don't recommend doing this, it is fun to know that social media can work both ways.

In 2015, three young women decided to commit cyber fraud against actual members of ISIS. These women contacted men affiliated with the terrorist group via social media and pretended they were interested in having personal relationships with them. On the Internet this is known as "catfishing," when someone pretends to be interested in another person, but their motives are other than what they claim. Oftentimes, catfishing is used to obtain money from their victims by perpetrating a fraud.

The women claimed they wanted to travel to Syria to join the war and marry ISIS fighters. The women further claimed the only thing stopping them was an inability to afford to travel. These inventive women even sent their would-be suitors fake pictures in order to better string the members of ISIS along. The ISIS fighters, believing they were about to gain both supporters and wives, wired the girls more than $3,000! After the money was transferred, the girls simply withdrew the funds, closed their bank accounts, and stopped all subsequent communication.

Again, I strongly advise against anyone ever communicating directly with dangerous criminals, let alone members of a terrorist organization. But it is certainly satisfying to know that these terrorists got scammed. However, I do highly recommend that you do the safe and lifesaving thing: if you spot something that seems like terror in social media, report it to police—before it's too late. That's what this book is all about.

One last thought on communication. While this chapter has focused on the use of social media, which is certainly pervasive within the ranks of terrorist organizations, let's not forget even the most basic, one-on-one verbal communication between two people. There are still the opportunities to overhear persons who decide to have a conversation to make plots and plans.

It was a 2009 chat between a terrorist and a law enforcement informant that prevented synagogues in the Bronx from being targeted for potential bombings. Likewise, in 2015, a driver in Mumbai, India, listened to terrorists openly discussing their deadly plans to plant a bomb while sitting in the backseat of his taxi. These passengers thought the significant traffic noise concealed their words, but luckily they were overheard and the driver notified police. An alert person listening to communicating terrorists foiled the terror attack.

As the saying goes, if you see something, say something. My advice is that it would also be wise to remember that if you hear something, or read something on social media, be sure to say something as well.

I-TIP: Pay attention to communications, in particular social media. Terrorists use social media to plan, recruit, lie, trick, and kill. We must spot their use of social media and report it to law enforcement.

CHAPTER FIVE

MONEY

**Terrorists need money for deadly acts against us.
We need to spot their movement of money and report it.**

*"Jihad needs very many things. Firstly (sic), it needs money.
Much is dependent on money today for jihad."*
—Omar Abu al-Chech*

Bullets cost money. Explosives aren't free and neither are guns. Cell phones, car and truck rentals, plane tickets, backpacks, shoes for shoe bombs, fake uniforms, bomb timers, meals, a place to sleep, even taking a shower all require financial ability. The heinous 9/11 terror killers spent thousands of dollars on flight lessons alone! They bought first-class airline seats, too. The money had to come from somewhere and move around to get into the hands of these and other terrorists.

Could we have spotted the terror money in action before the World Trade Center towers were left in ruin and thousands were killed or injured on 9/11? Could we have prevented the deaths and injuries caused in the 2015 San Bernardino attack during an innocent holiday party? Maybe someone could have prevented this carnage if they were alert enough to notice how the terrorists' money was moved and used and had the foresight to notify law enforcement. And "maybe" beats "nothing" when it comes to life and death.

---

*Omar Abu al-Chech is an ISIS commander.

America is the most charitable society on the planet. We are to be commended for helping worthy causes that touch our sympathies. But there is also cause for awareness and sometimes concern when terrorists use the façade of a charity, or even a so-called "church" or "temple," to attain or move cash. It is a real threat, and it is a major factor in financing terror in our homeland.

Take for example the Society of the Revival of Islamic Heritage. This society couldn't possibly have a connection to menacing terror detainees at Guantanamo, could it? This society even has a nice sounding and innocent title. They portray themselves as a nonprofit organization dedicated to preserving Islamic traditions and history. Our US State Department, however, has a very different view after investigating.

Purported activities discovered during the investigation of the "heritage society" have earned them a listing by the State Department as a terrorist-affiliated organization. And what are they doing in support of their terrorist brethren? Yes, you've got it. Money. The State Department says this group is providing financial support to persons affiliated with al-Qaeda.

So what should we all do? Try to spot bogus charities that might be in your community who are supposedly engaged in charitable purposes, but don't appear to do anything with the money raised.

Another fraud-infused charity front you might spot is a charity that doesn't raise money at all. There are certainly well-funded, legitimate charities that have no need to raise funds, such as those funded by the Bill and Melinda Gates or Mark Zuckerberg families. But most charities rely on donations, which is time-consuming and difficult for any legitimate charity. Be suspicious if you spot a charity that appears to have assets with no concern for dollars and they aren't expending efforts to seek donations. This is an indicator that they may be engaged in something illegal, including the next terror attack on your loved ones.

Terrorists really love the Internet. It's often used as their pathway to give us hell. Raising money, recruiting, and numerous fundraising activities can all involve the Internet. Capitalizing on the anonymity and fraudulent opportunities that the Internet provides such as hacking, fraudulent web sites, and more, terrorists attempt to raise and transfer funds using the worldwide web every day. Considering Americans spend an hour or more online every day on average, the opportunity to spot suspicious Internet activity as it relates to terrorist funding, and report it before it's too late, has real potential.

Terrorists will try to scam anyone they can. Brian Krebs, a former *Washington Post* reporter and author of the highly acclaimed online security forum KrebsonSecurity.com, recently reported an attempted hack on his personal PayPal account. A perpetrator tried to transfer funds from his account to a hacker group tied to the jihadist militant group ISIS.

You would think that terrorists seeking to commit cyber fraud would not want to tangle with someone as skilled and knowledgeable as Brian Krebs, who recognizes fraud when he sees it and knows just what to do. But while we may not all have that level of skill, we can still learn to be vigilant enough to prevent bad things from happening to our money, and from letting our money be unwittingly used to support terrorism.

Internet identity theft has been common in the United States for years, providing common criminals with a lucrative sources of income. The terrorists have taken notice and have learned that they can fund their own activities through the Internet, specifically with online identity theft.

Because these crimes occur online, they are often transnational; the perpetrators of these crimes are not just across state lines, but many times in faraway countries. This makes the job of tracking these criminals very difficult for law enforcement officials. Even when law enforcement is able to discover who might have committed the crime, these terrorists often reside in countries where United States law enforcement has little influence and US laws do not apply. Even when a criminal terrorist is tracked to a country that will work with US law enforcement agencies, the chance of recouping any stolen funds is limited.

Just as concerning is credit card fraud. Terrorists have found that the use of stolen credit cards is not only a way to fund their activities, but a convenient mechanism to move the funds quickly and conveniently without detection. This allows them to get money directly to the terrorists who need it for their plots and purchases.

Nevertheless, it is possible to spot identity theft and credit card fraud, and that's our opportunity to help catch the terrorists as they plan. Financial institutions need to be proactive in protecting their customers' information. We consumers need to be as well. Besides the cost and aggravation of being an identity theft victim, not protecting our personal info might be helping terrorists to pay for supplies to attack. It's about self-preservation and patriotic duty to help protect our nation.

According to the US Department of Labor, there are at least seven million Americans working in the financial industry in some capacity. That's about 7 percent of all full-time US workers. This means that, statistically, there are a fairly large number of us who are in position to spot terrorists raising, stealing, and moving money.

If you have a connection with the banking industry, investment firms, or any other entity that deals with the movement of money (such as employment with a wire transfer or check cashing business), there are several things to be aware of that would give rise to suspicion of criminal activity, which might very well also be financial support of terrorism.

Be heads up to spot things like unusual account deposits and withdrawals that aren't consistent with past account activity. If there is a large increase in dollars, where are these increased funds coming from all of a sudden? If the sudden influx of cash does not have a logical, legal explanation, then the logical, illegal explanation is one of criminality, and possibly terrorism.

Is there suddenly a high volume of wire transfers for a business that would normally not be engaged in such transactions? If you were operating a company with multiple offices and clients overseas, it would not be unusual to see multiple wire transfers on a regular basis. However, if the business is a small company with no logical connection to overseas operations, yet is making these sorts of wire transfers, it would be a good idea to notify the authorities. The same applies if these potentially fake businesses are moving funds to private citizens or to foreign banks as well.

Whether you are in a financial services business or not, you can be aware. As an example, ask yourself, "Why is that person buying unusual things with large amounts of cash, instead of using a credit card?"

When in doubt, if you spot something suspicious such as large sums of money being collected or moved, you can act as your company's security department; notify law enforcement.

The bottom line is terror requires money, and we need to do all we can to spot terrorists as they attain, use, and move money so that we can report it before it's too late.

I-TIP: Terrorists need money for deadly acts against us. We need to spot their use and movement of money and report it.

CHAPTER SIX

BAGS, PACKAGES, AND BACKPACKS

They hide bombs in bags and packages.
We need to spot suspicious items.

"The city was hit with a real terrorist attack executed in a frighteningly similar fashion. The real thing happened before we were able to execute."
—Unnamed Boston Police official*

A bomb hidden in airline-checked luggage. Innocent-looking backpacks containing bombs left on the sidewalk or in a café. Bomb packages mailed and dropped off. Bags of many varieties, appearing to be normal, are often the tools of terrorists in the homeland and across the world. These bags and packages can often be spotted before they detonate. We need to be aware and suspicious when we see unattended packages, backpacks, or actions as the terrorists prepare their deadly attacks.

It was a military-style camouflaged backpack that convicted domestic terrorist Eric Rudolph used to place a bomb at the Atlanta Olympics, killing one and injuring over one hundred unsuspecting individuals.

In another case, an alert citizen learned via the Internet that a backpack bomb loaded with nails—to inflict maximum human

---

*Unnamed Boston Police official quoted in the *Boston Globe*, discussing how prior to the Boston Marathon bombings the Department of Homeland Security had planned to conduct a training exercise involving the use of bombs inside of backpacks.

destruction—was to be placed at a public beach in Key West, Florida. Thankfully, the planned death and destruction was stopped because online extremist comments were spotted and reported to police by a vigilant American, before it was too late.

Maybe the Boston Marathon bomber brothers who used back-pack-delivered bombs could have been stopped before they killed. Surveillance video obtained by law enforcement, and used by the United States Attorney's Office at trial, show the Tsarnaev brothers walking down the street with backpacks slung over their shoulders. They then made their way onto Boylston Street, where the finish line for the Boston Marathon lay, from Gloucester Street, turning left and directly into the crowds. Later surveillance photos showed the backpacks were placed at their feet with numerous spectators around them, and even small children nearby. Later the brothers can be seen running from the area, along with everyone else, after the bombs within their backpacks exploded, killing three people and injuring 264 others.

In today's world, with the urgent need to be vigilant to terror actions, someone carrying a heavy backpack or bag, especially where it might seem out of place, should immediately raise concerns. Although the person carrying such a bag might be engaged in totally innocent behavior, we need to recognize that backpacks have become a vehicle for transporting and planting deadly devices. Similarly, if we spot someone leaving a backpack, bag, or package, or if we see one left unattended, we need to report it to the authorities immediately.

Israel, which has had to live under the threat of terrorism since the country's 1948 inception, has long recognized the dangers of explosives being concealed inside of backpacks or other luggage. Security within the country is extremely vigilant, constantly on the lookout for such potential threats, but even abroad those types of threats continue to plague the Israeli people. In 2012, an Israeli tour group, consisting mostly of students visiting Bulgaria, was attacked while inside their bus. A suicide bomber carried a backpack loaded with approximately six and a half pounds of TNT. It exploded, killing six people and injuring thirty-two others.

Authorities in the United States have become much more vigilant about inspecting bags and packages, and some have even taken the step of prohibiting carrying these items into places frequented by the public. Most sporting venues in the United States no longer permit backpacks, purses, coolers, or even foam-filled seat cushions into stadiums, fearing that these items may be concealing weapons of mass destruction. Instead, plastic see-through bags have become the rule for persons wishing to carry items with them, allowing for greater ease of inspection and making it virtually impossible to conceal dangerous items. Most people who attend sporting events and concerts now know this to be the rule. So, next time you are at a public event, if you see someone walking toward the crowd carrying one of these prohibited items, listen to your instincts. Do not approach the person; rather, immediately warn the authorities.

The reality is most businesses in the United States don't have much money to increase security, nor do many have strong security policies. These businesses can be prime targets for backpack and bag bombs. That's where we citizens come in. We need to be alert, vigilant, and suspicious to spot these packages of potential terror quickly in order to alert law enforcement officials in time. Be attentive to who is carrying what the next time you are in the movie theater, traveling by bus or train, at a local street festival, or in a busy shopping center, as terrorist security screening is virtually nonexistent in these places.

If you notice unattended bags, briefcases, or luggage, bring it to the immediate attention of law enforcement officials or security. Likewise, if during your commute you notice someone having trouble lifting what appears to be a heavy backpack, gym bag, or piece of luggage, this too might be a reason to become suspicious. It may be weighed down by a heavy explosive device, as opposed to being filled with innocent items such as clothing. During the March 2016 terrorist bombing in Belgium, one of the terrorists reportedly reprimanded a baggage handler minutes prior to the attack, telling the handler "don't touch my bags." Perhaps the terrorist's bag was extra heavy because it was packed with explosive materials and he thought it might arouse the handler's suspicion. Or maybe the terrorist feared the handler would accidentally set off the bomb before it was first placed in a crowded area in order to inflict the maximum amount of possible damage. Whatever the reason, in the future such words of admonishment should be considered as another possible indicator when viewed in the totality of the circumstances.

Also be very suspicious if traveling by train and, after having placed a heavy item in one compartment, the person then moves on to another compartment. Or, if you ever come across items that appear to be abandoned, this should be cause for immediate concern. It's your duty as a citizen to inform someone in charge. If that person doesn't take your concern seriously, talk to a police officer.

It is better to be safe than sorry when it comes to being suspicious about a potential bag or package bomb. If your intuition tells you something is wrong, especially in public locations or while you are traveling, listen to your instincts and let authorities know. By doing this you just might save your own life and others too.

I-TIP: They hide bombs in bags and packages. We need to spot suspicious packages and bags and alert authorities.

CHAPTER SEVEN

CLOTHING

Terrorists use clothing to hide bombs, weapons, and their identity. We must spot their out-of-place attire and report it.

*"I do have some tactical regrets of a sort . . . but
I don't regret losing my freedom."*
—Richard Reid*

It can be Halloween any day, or every day, for those in costume who desire to wreak terror upon us. Terrorists' clothes can be used to hide the true identity of the individual, as well as cover up tools of death and devastation. If we know a little about how clothing plays into the plots of terrorists, then we can have a chance to spot them before it's too late.

In places like Israel, and other countries where terror and safety are constant concerns, police and security personnel are trained to specifically look for things that seem out of place. Since terror has found us here in the homeland, as Americans we need to educate ourselves about the hard-learned experiences of other countries. In this case it's what the terrorists are doing with clothes. This can include clothing that does not seem right for the weather or occasion, or it might simply be that what the person is wearing is not consistent with their body type. Would a smaller, thinner person wear a particularly

---

*Richard Reid is a British-born attempted bomber who failed in his attempt to bring down an airliner by using explosives hidden in his shoe.

bulky down coat? It is a cause for concern because baggy clothing could be used to conceal weapons.

Think about this. You see someone with attire that just doesn't fit the circumstances. For example, it might not be particularly cold outside, but he or she (who is intent on terrorizing us) is wearing a heavy coat that could perhaps be concealing a suicide vest. Or there is not a cloud in the sky, but the person is wearing a long raincoat that could be concealing a long gun or rifle. Taking notice of how someone is dressed and see what is unusual or out of place, and then take action by immediately contacting law enforcement officials, which might mean the difference in preventing a terrorist attack.

These days we have to take off our shoes when we go through airport security because Richard Reid decided to conceal a bomb inside of one of his shoes. Reid earned the nickname "shoe-bomber" after attempting to kill himself and nearly two hundred passengers three days before Christmas in 2001.

In the immediate aftermath of 9/11, Reid was traveling aboard American Airlines Flight 63 bound for New York from Paris. With only about two hours remaining in the flight, an alert flight attendant smelled smoke and saw Reid using a match in an attempt to light a wire (as in fuse) that was protruding from one of his shoes. Imagine if another passenger had spotted Reid's shoe fuse sooner and reported it; his chances to kill would have been reduced even more so.

Fortunately, alerted by the flight attendant, nearby passengers jumped into action and were able to subdue Reid and restrain him for the remainder of the flight. Had they not done so, experts concluded, Reid's bomb would have blown a hole through the plane, killing everyone on board. For his actions Reid is serving a life sentence in the "Super Max" federal prison in Colorado. A big takeaway here is that it is not just jackets and such; we need to watch shoes and boots too.

Another thing we can learn from the Reid incident is how clothes can communicate. Just as we notice style on people, we can notice what's inappropriate or very unusual in a person's clothes. For example, Reid attempted to board a different plane a day earlier, but was delayed because airport officials thought he looked too disheveled in his appearance to be traveling on the flight. Reid was dressed sloppily, his hair was all tattered, and he appeared to be dirty. This delay, because officials thought something was amiss, caused Reid to miss his original flight. Had Reid boarded this earlier flight, who knows if anyone would have noticed as he attempted to light the fuse on the bomb he was carrying.

Another example could be seen in the March 2016 Belgium bombing at the Brussels airport. On the airport surveillance video the two bombers are observed to be wearing only one glove, using the gloved hand to push their luggage carts that carried the explosives. Experts believe the terrorists may have worn the single gloves to prevent static electricity from being accidentally transmitted from their hands to the detonators, which could have triggered a premature explosion. As a result of the actions of these terrorists in the Belgium attack, should you observe someone wearing one glove in such an unusual manner, in conjunction with crowds and transporting items, this should be recognized as a serious potential indicator of terrorism and necessitate action by immediately warning the authorities.

Another example of how dress can be a potential threat indicator occurred here in the United States on July 4, 2002. Hesham Mohamed Hadayet, a forty-one-year-old Egyptian national, entered Los Angeles International Airport and proceeded directly to the El Al ticket counter. As he approached, Hadayet pulled out a gun and opened fire, killing two people and wounding four others before he was fatally shot by an El Al security official. Fortunately, El Al security saw Hadayet enter the airport and his appearance made them suspicious. So, even before Hadayet began shooting, security had been heading his way to intercept him.

One of the signs noted by security was that even though it was a warm July day, Hadayet was still wearing a coat to conceal his gun. Besides the way Hadayet was dressed, security noticed that something was missing: luggage.

Hadayet entered the airport and walked directly to the ticket counter, but was carrying neither luggage nor a carry-on bag. The coat in warm weather and lack of any bags were key indicators for security to decide that this person should be given a closer look. Although Hadayet was able to fire several shots before being killed, it could have been much worse had vigilant security not spotted his clothing and lack of luggage.

More recently, Paris experienced one of Europe's worst terrorist attacks. It began when one of three attackers approached entrance door "J" to the Stade de France, where a soccer match was under way. Although the attacker had a ticket to the match, he was wearing a particularly heavy coat, which reportedly aroused the suspicions of security. Believing that he could be concealing some type of contraband, the attacker was turned away. The attacker walked a few feet away and then detonated his suicide belt hidden under his coat. Two others who had been working with the original attacker then detonated their hidden suicide belts. So began the night of attacks in Paris that ended with 129 people killed and another 350 injured.

Were it not for stadium security being vigilant and denying him access to the stadium, many more people could have been killed or injured. Remember, there is never going to be enough security or police to spot everything; all of us must be vigilant and report our suspicions to law enforcement officials.

During that night in Paris there were coordinated terrorist attacks at seven different locations, carried out by three separate teams of attackers, totaling nine attackers in all. Clothing worn by these terrorists, in some cases, helped Parisian authorities identify and take them down. The way the attackers were dressed was enough to make them stand out, and this valuable information was relayed by witnesses to the authorities.

The attackers at locations other than the stadium appeared as if they were wearing military uniforms. Their clothing was described as tight-fitting black jumpers with no zippers or collars visible, black boots, and in some cases matching wool caps. It is noteworthy that unlike those dressed in heavy clothing to conceal weapons, or even Richard Reid trying to hide a bomb in his shoe, these terrorists were dressed tactically so that clothing would not get in their way or hinder their movement or use of weapons in their attacks.

Seeing someone dressed like these Paris attackers you might initially ask yourself if they are simply fashion challenged. But, in light of the Paris attacks, you need to also consider the deadly alternative. Furthermore, if there are multiple individuals dressed alike, it may be an indicator that there is cause for real concern.

The saying goes that clothes makes the man. In some cases clothing might also make the terrorist. Pay attention to what people are wearing, and take note of anything you think is out of place or suspicious. It might be nothing or it could be you're spotting little clues just in time to give law enforcement the upper hand in preventing an attack before it's too late.

I-TIP: Terrorists use clothing to hide bombs, weapons, and identity. We must spot their out-of-place attire and report it.

CHAPTER EIGHT

SUSPICIOUS VEHICLES

Terrorists use cars and trucks to attack. We must spot the vehicles they use and tell police before it is too late.

"The impact of terrorism, not merely on individual nations, but on humanity as a whole, is intrinsically evil, necessarily evil, and wholly evil."
—*Benjamin Netanyahu**

No one could have imagined that a typical SUV parked in New York City was a bomb on wheels. Is that ambulance really an emergency vehicle or a cover for terrorists about to deliver death? Unfortunately, we live in a terror world, and that means just about everything we see in our daily lives can be suspect, including the cars and trucks we see around us.

Times Square in New York City is one of the most popular tourist destinations in the world, which is why a terrorist planned an attack there in May 2010.

While selling t-shirts on the street, an alert vendor spotted smoke coming from a parked SUV. He also noticed other indicators: the vehicle was parked awkwardly at the curb and the vehicle's emergency flashers were on. The vendor immediately notified a nearby New York

---

*Benjamin Netanyahu is the Prime Minister of Israel.

43

City police officer, who checked the scene and immediately realized he was dealing with a terrorist situation. Times Square was quickly evacuated, which meant thousands of people had to be moved from the area. At the same time the bomb squad was called in.

Authorities determined the SUV contained a makeshift bomb consisting of gunpowder, gasoline, and three 20-gallon tanks of propane. Had this bomb gone off it would have erupted into a massive fireball resulting in massive casualties. Fortunately, none of that happened, due in large part to the vendor who saw something was not right and notified police before it was too late.

Faisal Shahzad, a thirty-year-old Pakistan-born resident of Bridgeport, Connecticut, was arrested as he attempted to board an international flight to the Middle East. Law enforcement officials identified their subject by tracing the SUV to the original owner who had sold the vehicle on Craigslist to Shahzad. Echoing what was written in chapter 4 on social media, Shahzad used the Internet to acquire what he needed to engage in terrorism. He also used a fake ID for impersonation, as discussed in chapter 3.

Upon arrest Shahzad admitted planting the car bomb and that he trained for the mission at a Pakistani terrorist training camp.

Of course not every terrorist vehicle is going to have smoke coming out of it and be improperly parked, making it easier to spot. However, as you can see there were other indicators, and there usually will be, to allow you to spot what is out of the ordinary.

Think back to the story of Timothy McVeigh, who parked the rented box truck outside of the federal building in Oklahoma City. In 1995, you might have been able to park a vehicle like he did in front of a government building without anyone being concerned. But not anymore. Most of the streets in front of government buildings and major offices are now no-parking zones, and crash-proof concrete barriers have been installed around the perimeters.

The indicator for you is if you see an unattended vehicle that seems suspicious, follow your instincts and notify the authorities. There is nothing to lose if it is an innocent vehicle. If that vehicle is an instrument of terror, then you may well have just saved lives. This is particularly true when the unattended vehicle is parked next to a military facility, government building, power plant, shopping mall, hotel, stadium, or school.

Another indicator to consider is how the terrorist acquires the vehicle for the planned attack. In some cases the vehicles might be stolen, but in many other instances vehicles are obtained legally. It could be a rental, such as in the 1993 World Trade Center bombing, or a purchase like the Craigslist example cited earlier.

Here's how you or those you know can help spot a terror vehicle situation before it's too late. If you work somewhere that rents, works on, cleans, or services vehicles, or any other activity that gives you access to vehicles, you may be in a position to observe indicators of terror.

Is the person who is renting the vehicle reluctant to provide their personal information to complete the transaction? Is the customer paying cash and leaving a large deposit instead of using a credit or debit card as most people do? If and when the vehicle is returned does the customer recall the correct name used when it was rented? You know what your name is when you rent a vehicle and you know what your name is when you return it. You might be surprised to learn that criminals and terrorists don't always pay attention to the small details like what name they used for a reservation.

Those who service vehicles have an opportunity to spot indicators such as burn marks, or items in the vehicle like large amounts of fireworks, propane tanks, or flammable liquids—any or all of which could be an indication that the vehicle might have been used in a terror test run. (There is more on this subject in chapter 11.)

Also, keep a sharp eye out to spot blueprints or photographs of important buildings, landmarks, military facilities, malls, etc., as the terrorist may have left behind maps indicating where they are plotting to attack.

Anything left behind, such as extremist literature, receipts for hazardous material purchases, or certainly any actual weapons, ammunition, or explosives, could be an indicator of potential terror activities. If you see any of these indicators, contact law enforcement.

Finally, there is always the possibility of what the law enforcement community refers to as "cloned" vehicles. They are cars and trucks that have been disguised to look like police, fire, or other official vehicles, but in fact they are fake.

You have probably seen former police cars and ambulances that have been taken out of service with their markings removed, which are now being driven by private citizens. Shockingly, but true, nothing prevents a would-be terrorist from purchasing one of these retired vehicles and turning it into a bomb-laden weapon that looks "official." In 2015, Germany's Hannover Stadium avoided carnage among fans when an ambulance full of explosives was found to be a bogus emergency vehicle.

For us here in the United States, we need to take note of any emergency vehicles that just don't seem right. Do the law enforcement emblems appear mismatched or improperly placed? Does the model vehicle appear to be different from that of other police vehicles currently in use in the city? If you spot a suspicious emergency or official-appearing vehicle, let police know before it is too late.

Trust your instincts. No one knows better than you whether something just does not seem right. As we have all heard since 9/11, and repeated throughout this book, if you see something, say something.

I-TIP: Terrorists use cars and trucks to attack. We must spot the vehicles they use and tell police before it is too late.

CHAPTER NINE

SABOTAGE

Terrorists try to sabotage our safety, security, and technology to disrupt and kill. We must spot terrorist sabotage before it's too late.

"It is very important to concentrate on hitting the US economy through all means possible."

—*Osama bin Laden**

The dictionary definition of *sabotage* is "to deliberately damage or destroy." Terrorists use sabotage with the goal of creating chaos, social disruption, and destruction of our basic infrastructure (power plants, communications, and water systems), or even aircraft in flight. Imagine if you couldn't access the Internet, pump gas for your car, or get money from the bank. These are real-life examples of what terrorist sabotage can do to us.

To commit sabotage terrorists prepare by planning, acquiring supplies, gaining access to secure places and communicating with their co-conspirators. These actions are indicators that enable us to spot sabotage in the making before disaster strikes.

In much of this book I have concentrated on profiling terrorist actions so we can report them to law enforcement officials before an attack occurs. We've looked at how they communicate and the clothes they wear, etc. I have also shared the importance of noticing

*Osama bin Laden was the founder of al-Qaeda and mastermind of the September 11, 2001, attacks on the United States homeland.

out-of-place objects, such as abandoned backpacks and suspicious vehicles. Sometimes, though, it is neither a person nor a thing that you can spot. It might just be noticing something that has been tampered with for the purpose of a terrorist act.

Osama bin Laden publicly proclaimed that al-Qaeda's objective was to target key sectors of the US economy. Therefore, sabotage committed by terrorists might not be as obvious as wires protruding from an electrical box, or oil leaking from a container, although don't discount the possibility of those things either. Remember Richard Reid, the convicted shoe bomber, had a fuse protruding from his shoe, not just to bring down an airline, but also to create fear among the traveling public in order to compromise the commercial airline industry. Likewise, such attacks might include targeting electric power facilities by sabotaging various safety and performance systems.

Over the past ten years various terrorist groups have conducted approximately 2,500 attacks around the world against power lines, electrical towers, and power substations, causing disruption to services in varying degrees. Just one day after the Boston Marathon bombing sabotage hit a California power plant. In the dark of night unknown snipers opened fire on a power substation, knocking out seventeen transformers and disrupting electrical service. Disrupting our normal way of life has long been the objective of terrorist organizations.

Many parts of infrastructure in the United States are susceptible to attack—typically with little risk to the attacker. Terrorists know this all too well, and they continue to try to exploit it.

Rural and wilderness areas are where many power transmission lines, power substations, communications facilities, natural gas supplies, and generating facilities are located. These are commonly referred to as "high-value targets," which, if damaged or destroyed, would significantly impact our everyday life and put us at added risk because of the loss of fundamental systems and services.

Nobody intends to make it easier for the terrorists to find our vital systems to plan an attack, but the reality is anyone can get detailed maps of US power and communication systems from the Internet. Satellite data and photos can be purchased by virtually anyone to plan an attack. In addition, terrorists can position themselves on the ground near power, communications, and water facilities to observe and take photos as they plan their terror attacks. As the power plant snipers in California proved, fences and guards are not a complete solution to protect against an attack.

Whether it's an act of vandalism, or something more sinister, is not really the question. All that truly matters is that we question what we see and be ready to spot the indicators and report it to law enforcement right away.

Hikers, cross-country skiers, horseback riders, those who enjoy all-terrain vehicles, and many others, are often in remote areas near the vicinity of electrical towers, power stations, and other critical components of our infrastructure. This is an opportunity to spot possible attempts at terror sabotage. By being aware that these sites are terrorist targets, you can be alert and mentally prepared to recognize anything unusual.

Perhaps someone will notice damage from a previously unsuccessful attempt to bring down an electrical tower. It's happened before: at the Bonneville power plant in Oregon, someone tampered with the bolts that hold the tower in place. Another example is in Santa Cruz, California, where 92,000 residents had little or no electricity for two days after an unknown group toppled a PG&E power pole.

When it comes to sabotage of our country's critical infrastructure, the threats are not solely limited to the electrical power grid, and the consequences can be even more serious. In 2012, NBC News reported that San Onofre nuclear power plant in Southern California discovered that one of the plant's generators had been sabotaged by tampering. Someone poured engine coolant into an oil system of one of the backup diesel generators, which disabled it. While this act alone would not cause a "China syndrome" meltdown (or Russia's Chernobyl or Japan's Fukushima), it should make us all nervous to know that someone with authorized access to a nuclear power plant engaged in the purposeful act of sabotage. This act of sabotage was committed by an *insider*. It is bad enough that we have to be on guard against those who are seeking to infiltrate and destroy, but we must also be ready to spot the malicious insider with the potential to hurt us for whatever reason their motivation to do so may be. The point is, whether at work or play, there are good reasons to be alert to indicators of sabotage, even if it is within a controlled environment.

Cyber intrusions like hacking are essentially a form of sabotage through the use of a computer. Frighteningly, cyber attacks have become so commonplace that we barely pay attention anymore when we hear of these events. This leaves us more vulnerable and is a dangerous trend.

Whether it is our critical infrastructure, or some other form of a cyber intrusion that can impact our families and our entire economy, we cannot dismiss the possibility that the intrusion might be an attempt to further terrorist aims.

In many cases those within the company whose job it is to defend against these attacks are able to quickly limit the damages. Unfortunately, due to the fear of bad press, many companies are reluctant to report these types of attacks to law enforcement. Companies may be fearful of damage to their public image, thinking it's more important to protect their image than to notify law enforcement that an incident has occurred. Also companies might think, "Why bother calling the police?" if they were able to stop the attack and no real damage occurred.

Companies need to rethink this "keep it secret" viewpoint. With my twenty plus years in law enforcement, you can be assured that law enforcement is not in the business of talking to the media about ongoing investigations. It's often said that the FBI invented the phrase "No comment." Companies don't need to worry about an investigation harming their public image. What is reported to law enforcement authorities will remain confidential.

Businesses need to understand it is important to bring these matters to the attention of law enforcement officials. This allows the authorities to have situational awareness of what has happened so they can warn other businesses of the potential for such an attack, all the while maintaining your company's privacy. Likewise, law enforcement may already be investigating these matters based upon similar attacks on other businesses. You never know if a tiny piece of evidence from one company's sabotage might just be the missing clue law enforcement needs to identify who is responsible. It has happened many times in a variety of different business and industries. Sharing this information becomes a civic duty, and may very well be a matter of your survival.

A cyber attack might sound like a benign form of sabotage when compared to disrupting generators of a nuclear power plant or attempting to knock down electrical towers and power lines, but these computer intrusions can also be deadly. Sabotage was behind a giant gas pipeline explosion in Turkey in 2008. A hacker entered the computer network and made changes to the system that caused the explosion.

Like Turkey, the United States has millions of miles of pipelines that distribute everything from oil and hazardous liquids to natural gas and chemicals, all of which can be vulnerable to cyber attacks by sabotaging computer networks. Whether you work in information technology, or if you're the CEO, businesses need to understand the critical importance of reporting these attacks to law enforcement officials.

Finally, another form of sabotage is product tampering. When those words are used it reminds many of the 1982 Chicago Tylenol tampering case.

After taking what they thought was extra-strength Tylenol, seven people died because the product had been laced with potassium cyanide. To this day this case remains unsolved, but it highlights the importance of spotting and reporting the possible sabotage of anything we eat or drink. Food and drink don't just impact our direct health either; they're a large part of our economy.

Imagine biting into a piece of fruit contaminated with toxic mercury. It happened in Israel when the Arab Revolutionary Council used liquid mercury to sabotage fruit being exported from Israel to Europe. Not only did this cause a dozen people to become sick, it created fear of purchasing Israeli produce, which seriously impacted the country's sales and exports.

England has also been a victim of terror sabotage, and it could have affected us here in the homeland. Consumers there found metal shards in potatoes purchased at the store. England had to quickly invest in costly metal detection equipment in order to examine vegetable products consumed there and shipped around the world, including into the United States.

In both the Israel and England cases, consumers were injured as were the economies of those countries. This one form of sabotage sadly had life-and-death, as well as major economic impacts.

If you work in any part of our country's critical infrastructure, you have an opportunity to help yourself and the entire community by spotting indicators of sabotage. If something appears to have been tampered with or sabotaged, it just may be terror in action.

Clearly, sabotage can happen in many different ways, from the food we eat to the technology we rely on every day to go through life. Keep your eyes open, and question the unusual or what doesn't seem right. In other words, try to spot sabotage and report it. Even if the attempt of sabotage failed, it should still be reported to the authorities. Your reporting just might prevent a future successful attack.

I-TIP: Terrorists try to sabotage our safety, security, and technology to disrupt and kill. We must spot terrorist sabotage before it's too late.

CHAPTER TEN

TEST RUNS

**Terrorists use test runs to ensure their success
of achieving death and destruction.
We must spot the terrorist test run and report it.**

*"The attack by the Islamic State in America is only
the beginning of our efforts."*
—**Abu Ibrahim Al-Amriki***

Auto companies test-drive their vehicles. Actors rehearse their performances. New stores and restaurants have pre-opening days where they test their employees' skills and how well operations are working. Our police and military conduct drills before being deployed to ensure good planning, that their gear is in working order, and that they will prevail against the criminal or event threat.

Ominously, terrorists also conduct "drills" that the law enforcement community refers to as "test runs." These test runs oftentimes provide a myriad of indicators for you to spot.

A test run is essentially a practice run, a rehearsal carried out by the terrorists so that they can determine whether their planned actions are going to be successful. Like practice is to an athlete, the test run allows the terrorists to practice their movements and timing, to memorize what steps to take, and to ascertain if they are going to encounter any difficulties standing in the way.

---

*Abu Ibrahim Al-Amriki is an alleged US-born ISIS terrorist.

The test run might also be for the purpose of testing the strength or weaknesses of security personnel, monitoring the response times of law enforcement by calling in false alarms, identifying additional obstacles they might not have considered, or simply timing how long an attack will take to carry out.

My experience in law enforcement tells me that after all other necessary preparation has been completed, the smart, well-trained and determined terrorist is going to conduct a test run of the attack upon our safety and freedom. We must be far more aware of this methodology, and that's why I am devoting this entire chapter to the topic.

One test run that was thought to have occurred prior to 9/11 involved two Saudi Arabian doctoral students who were studying in the United States at the University of Arizona. Hamdan Alshalawi and Muhammed AlQudahieen boarded a flight from Phoenix bound for Washington, DC, with a connecting flight to the Middle East. During the first leg, the two individuals reportedly asked the flight attendants a number of questions about airline security, creating suspicion among flight personnel.

At some point during the flight, AlQudahieen got up from his assigned seat and walked to the cockpit door, which he then attempted to open. This possible test of the cockpit door, in combination with the unusual security questions, created enough concern that the pilot elected to make an unscheduled landing. The pilot landed the plane at the Port Columbus International Airport, full of passengers, far from the terminal. Passengers were then instructed to evacuate the plane.

Alshalawi and AlQudahieen were handcuffed, detained by police, and subsequently questioned for several hours by the FBI. The two were later released based on lack of evidence of "intent" to commit a crime. However, the next day, Alshalawi and AlQudahieen held a press conference where they threatened to file a lawsuit against the airline, alleging they were "humiliated" and that the airline acted "prematurely and without evidence." AlQudahieen explained that he had only been looking for the airplane restroom, and confused it with the cockpit door.

So was this an overreaction by the airline crew for an innocent mistake, or was it a terror test run? We may never know for sure, but we do know that during the course of their living and studying in the United States, Alshalawi and AlQudahieen had made numerous flights to and from their home country of Saudi Arabia. A logical assumption would be that with all of their prior flying experiences, they should know the difference between the cockpit door and the airplane restroom.

If this were in fact a pre-9/11 test run, the purpose might have been to ascertain the level of security on board planes at the time, including whether the cockpit door was locked during flight. Also the fact that these students made a public announcement that they were considering a lawsuit so quickly raised suspicions about their true intentions.

Perhaps their goal was to discourage the US air carriers from being confrontational with foreign travelers, even if they are engaging in suspicious activity. If the actions of these two individuals were based solely upon their own ignorance, the circumstances witnessed by the flight crew are identical to what actual test runs might look like. Threats of lawsuits should never stop us from being aware of possible indicators of terrorism and reporting it so that it can be properly investigated.

A separate, well-documented pre-9/11 event involved the award-winning and Oscar-nominated actor James Woods. He encountered some of the actual terrorists on a flight a month prior to our homeland being attacked.

During a flight from Boston to Los Angeles, Mr. Woods reported that he observed four Middle Eastern men acting in what he considered to be a suspicious manner. The men, who were seated in first-class, did not do anything to pass the time during the long cross-country flight. They did not eat, drink, sleep, or engage in any sort of business work, as most traveling passengers would do. For the entire flight these four individuals reportedly just stared straight ahead, only occasionally speaking with one another.

Concerned, Mr. Woods eventually approached the one of the flight attendants and quietly shared his observations. The attendant purportedly told Mr. Woods they had noted the same peculiarities and had informed the flight crew.

Although the flight landed without incident, this information must have been documented in some manner by the airline, because the morning after 9/11, Mr. Woods was awakened by a phone call from the FBI. The special agent who was calling told Mr. Woods that he and another agent were outside his home and wanted to speak with him about his flight to Los Angeles. In probably the only moment of levity during the events of 9/11, the actor asked the special agent how they had gotten his address and phone number. The agent replied, "Mr. Woods, after all we are the FBI."

The general consensus in law enforcement circles is that this Boston to Los Angeles flight was a test run of the 9/11 terrorist attack. Actor James Woods did exactly what we all need to do. He spotted something that he thought was suspicious and reported it.

Another form of a test run may be a terrorist planning to place a bomb contained in a backpack or duffle bag. The terrorist may conduct a test run by leaving a backpack or luggage, filled only with clothes, in a public area of an airport or hotel to see if it's noticed. If the bag just sits there without any security official investigating, the terrorist knows the test run has been a success. They can plant their device, leaving it to detonate and kill.

If planning to use a vehicle to plant a bomb, the terrorist will want to know how long the vehicle can be parked before security or law enforcement takes action. If no one spots and reports the vehicle, especially if it is parked illegally or in a suspicious location, the test run will have confirmed for the terrorist the likelihood of a successful planned attack.

False alarms are another form of a test run for terrorists. They want to know how long it will take for first responders to arrive. The problem for law enforcement is that a false alarm is not an unusual event.

Police officers respond to calls every day that turn out to be false alarms. Sometimes people will accidentally dial 9-1-1 and, suddenly recognizing their error, just hang up. Believe it or not, some people actually think it is funny to purposefully dial 9-1-1 and hang up. How are the police to know if it is just an accidental or prank 9-1-1 call, or a terrorist test run? The difference can be in spotting indicators and sharing this information with police.

First responders need to respond to everything. That's why the rest of us must be the eyes and ears to help to see the indicators. We need to be on the lookout to spot a decoy or test vehicle, or the leaving of an "innocent" test duffel bag, in a densely populated area.

As the other chapters in this book tell you (particularly chapters 6 and 8), there are many steps before the test run and those steps, from buying supplies to odd behaviors in routine situations, are opportunities to spot and report.

The police may not be aware of what other activities have occurred at a particular location when responding to a false alarm, but you may have seen additional indicators that, when added together, tell you something might be a possible terrorist test run.

Has someone been taking pictures of the building or asking questions about security that seemed out of the ordinary? Has anyone been sitting for long periods of time in a nearby parked car, perhaps conducting surveillance? All of these actions, along with the false alarm, might just be indicators of a terrorist test run. Spotting and reporting your observations, combined with the knowledge of a false alarm, might be the key to preventing a terrorist attack.

One final thought when keeping your eyes open to indicators of a terrorist test run is to think about the date on the calendar. Terrorists have been known to conduct their attacks to coincide with specific anniversaries. For example, the attack in Benghazi, Libya, occurred on September 11, 2012, to coincide with the 9/11 attacks eleven years earlier. Likewise, also think about the holidays that are important to us in the United States, Christmas and New Year's, along with patriotic celebrations such as Memorial Day and the Fourth of July, as these can be attractive occasions for terrorists planning attacks. If you witness something that might be an indicator of a test run, upcoming calendar dates might give you further reason for concern and all the more reason to tell law enforcement.

To practice and gauge their chances of success, terrorists will conduct a test run of their operation before an attack. Look for the indicators and don't hesitate to share with law enforcement what you have spotted.

I-TIP: Terrorists use test runs to ensure their success of achieving death and destruction. We must spot the terrorist test run and report it.

On patrol at the San Diego-Mexico border, circa 1993.

Iannarelli with Police of Chief, Jerry Sanders, in San Diego, 1993.

FBI Director Louis Freeh swears in FBI Special Agent John G. Iannarelli, 1995.

FBI Director Louie Freeh and Assistant Director Paul Phillip look on as Iannarelli presents to graduating FBI agents about the Oklahoma City bombing and the growing terrorist and other dangers facing law enforcement, 1995.

JGI conducting surveillance, circa 1996.

Within two years of swear-in FBI Special Agent Iannarelli is presented the FBI's Distinguished Service Award by the Director Louie Freeh, 1996.

On the FBI range maintaining firearms tactical proficiency with Special Agent Michael Boady.

With the Detroit FBI SWAT Team after a takedown of the Outlaws biker gang, circa 1997.

Four days before the terror attacks of September 11, 2001, Iannarelli was formally recognized by FBI Director Muller at a national law enforcement conference.

Iannarelli covering the President's visit to the FBI Academy's Laboratory in Quantico, Virginia, with press office representative Ed Cogswell, 2003.

On assignment in New York City for Super Bowl XLVIII, 2014.

With the "real" FBI mob undercover operative made famous with the film *Donnie Brasco*, Joseph D. Pistone.

Iannarelli is thanked by Pope Francis after a formal security presentation to Vatican leadership and their security officials in Rome, circa 2013.

Feeling great near the top of the nearly-completed Freedom Tower at the World Trade Center in New York, 2014.

CHAPTER ELEVEN

IF TERROR FINDS YOU

They come to kill us. We must spot them, escape, hide, call 9-1-1, and, if necessary, fight back.

"Bad things happen to good people, and when you're facing terrorism . . . you can have every wonderful plan in place, but I am a realist."

—*Warren Rudman**

Who could have imagined that four marines and a sailor would be gunned down by a terrorist on a street in America in July 2015?

Only the terrorists who were involved knew there was going to be an attack on innocents at the San Bernardino County Department of Public Health in December 2015. Sadly, twelve innocent Americans and twenty-two others were injured when the killing couple attacked.

These are cases where unsuspecting Americans fell victim to terrorist attacks right here on our homeland. Hopefully you and your loved ones never experience this, but the world is a dangerous place, and we must be prepared if terror finds us. Of course spotting terrorist activity before it's too late is ideal, but life doesn't always provide us with ideal scenarios—despite everything that has been presented in the previous ten chapters to empower you to spot terror and report it.

The unfortunate reality is that there will be future attacks, and while it's painful to say, you might just find yourself in the middle of

*Warren Rudman is a former US Senator (New Hampshire).

one. Therefore, this chapter is all about surviving should a terrorist attack find you, your loved ones, or you and your coworkers on the job.

The first step in planning is for you to consider how you might respond in the immediate aftermath of a terrorist event. Does your family have a meeting plan? How will you account for everyone in your family and ensure they are all safe if something were to occur?

You might think that you'll simply telephone one another, but don't count on that being foolproof. During 9/11, the entire phone infrastructure was so overloaded that thousands of calls could not get through. Added to that was a mass exodus from New York and Washington as businesses abruptly closed and people headed home seeking safety from this real-life disaster. You can imagine the great volume of traffic on the roadways and, at the same time, people were flocking to mass transit systems, yet bus and train lines were shutting down. It could all happen again.

Discuss with your loved ones what you will do in the event of a terror disaster. You will first attempt to reach one another by telephone call, text, or even e-mail. Depending upon the size of your family you may want to go so far as to decide who will contact whom and in what order. For example, Mom might contact the oldest daughter, while Dad will try and connect with the oldest son, and both parents will continue reaching out as pre-planned. By having this emergency contact list, your entire family can be accounted for in a much faster and more organized manner, as opposed to having everyone scrambling to contact one another and overlapping efforts with other family members.

Keep in mind that your phones may not work, and even if they do, you will still want to have a designated meeting place so the family can be brought together. While it's more than likely the meeting place will be your home, it is important to also determine in advance a secondary location in case the incident prevents travel back to your family residence. If your home was in lower Manhattan when 9/11 occurred, it made sense to seek shelter elsewhere in order to stay clear of the emergency crews and people fleeing the area.

In addition to a designated meeting place, your family should also have an evacuation plan should you need to relocate temporarily after the incident. Decide where you will go and how you will get there, remembering that mass transit might be disrupted and the roads will be crowded with cars resulting in traffic and delays. Likewise, if the power is out you won't be able to purchase fuel for your vehicle, so the distance you can travel might be limited. Furthermore, think about the things you would need to take with you during relocation such as medications, food, clothing for the weather, etc.

Once your family has relocated, stay apprised of further potential threats. Monitor the news through television, radio (battery operated), or the Internet to learn what significant developments may have occurred, including whether your area of relocation is deemed safe, and when you can return home. Don't take any unnecessary chances; instead, defer to those in authority regarding your movements.

Once you have a family plan for how everyone will respond immediately after a terror incident, take the time to discuss the plan as a family and then schedule review and practice using your emergency contact list to ensure everyone understands their roles and what needs to be done should terror find you.

Other than understanding the importance of having an emergency response plan for your family, the other major component of incident planning is to know what to do to survive if you find yourself in the middle of an actual terror attack.

For bombings there isn't much you can do during the initial blast. This is why so much emphasis has been placed on spotting the indicators of terror to prevent such things from happening when possible. Sadly, when it comes to bombings, luck comes into play to a certain degree. Will you be within the radius of the blast zone or far enough away to escape without physical injury? However, once the bomb has gone off, the danger is still far from over, and there is now a need for you to take immediate action.

Be aware of the possibility of secondary explosive devices, which in law enforcement terms means additional bombs that have been set to go off later, sometimes in a matter of minutes. That's because terrorists know that the first responders will be coming to the rescue. In many cases terrorists have specifically targeted first responders with secondary devices in an attempt to injure or kill these brave individuals. Just as disconcerting, terrorists also know that the public will immediately try to flee the targeted area. The terrorists' goal is to inflict more death and damage by placing these secondary devices where they expect logical routes of evacuation.

Keep these secondary devices in mind, should a bomb attack occur, and get yourself and your loved ones to safety by leaving the area immediately and retreating to some place that would be a probable area of safety. Beyond immediate safety, if you think you have information or may have spotted something that might help law enforcement (perhaps you even saw the bomber), get yourself to safety first, do so quickly, and then contact the police.

Only a minor delay in time of sharing your information with the authorities is recommended—literally only by a few moments. If you remain in the immediately area of the attack you might become a victim yourself if there is a secondary explosion. The information you have will not do law enforcement any good if you are not alive to provide it. Unless you literally know who the bomber is and see him or her running away, get to safety first and then share whatever information you might have with authorities.

You may consider remaining behind if there were others who were injured and in need of immediate medical attention and you are capable of offering such assistance. If the professional responders are not yet on the scene, or the attack was to such a degree that the responders are overwhelmed with casualties, then it is understandable to answer the instinct to help others.

We saw this in the aftermath of the Boston Marathon bombings when many of the brave spectators and runners, even though warned of the possibility of secondary devices, remained to help the critically injured, uncertain as to whether they were putting their own lives at additional risk, and no doubt saving many lives in the process.

In such a circumstance remaining at the attack location is not only understandable, but is also commendable. However, remember that by remaining behind you are still at further risk. So now the objective becomes to remove yourself as soon as possible, along with the victim you are helping, as soon as it's physically and medically safe to do so.

Other than detonating a bomb, the other most notable terrorist action that poses a significant threat to the general public is what law enforcement refers to as an "active shooter." An active shooter is defined as an individual actively engaged in killing or attempting to kill people, generally choosing to do so in populated areas.

Although typically using a handgun or rifle, an active shooter can also use any type of weapon to inflict casualties. In 2014 a former employee, who had been radicalized while incarcerated in prison, entered an Oklahoma food packing plant with a knife and attacked. He beheaded one employee and seriously injured another before he was shot. In both Paris and San Bernardino during 2015 we saw terrorists who used pistols and long guns. Also in 2015 a terrorist with a knife attacked passengers aboard a train from Amsterdam to France, only to be stopped when three heroic American passengers subdued the attacker.

Sadly, over the years we have seen an increase in the number of active shooter cases. Although the focus of this book has been on terrorism, an active shooter may be motivated to commit these crimes for a number of reasons. These reasons can include hatred, prejudice, mental illness, to facilitate the commission of a crime and getaway, as a disgruntled employee who is determined to deliver "payback" to an employer, or a domestic violence situation, along with a variety of other potential reasons.

As there are so many distorted motivations for these attacks, active shooting situations have materialized in numerous locations such as schools, offices, churches, shopping malls, and movie theaters, etc. Because active shooting situations can happen anywhere, it is important that you are ready to respond wherever you may be.

Just as importantly, statistically active shootings are over before law enforcement even arrives on the scene. Sometimes the shooter will flee the area before the police get there, as was the case in San Bernardino, or the active shooter might take his or her own life, as several of the attackers did in Paris. You must therefore be prepared to respond to an active shooting situation with the knowledge that you may be on your own until the incident is over.

The immediate response to an active shooting is simple: you should run away if it is possible to do so. In situations where running away is not possible, then you should hide. If presented with circumstances where neither running nor hiding is an option, then you should take on the attacker and fight.

Before examining each of these three options and when they should be used, it is important to remember there is no single answer or response for every single attack. Each situation for each person will be different. Some persons may have a disability that would prevent them from running away. Others may find themselves in an area without a place to properly hide. Still others may not be physically capable of mounting a defense. But pretending the situation does not exist will not help either. You cannot save yourself or others by hoping for mercy from the attacker. Hence, you need to think about your options and make the decision that is best given your abilities and the set of circumstances with which you find yourself presented.

If available as an option, running away from the danger should be your first course of action when presented with an active shooter situation. If you work in an office or attend school, think in advance of the logical escape routes and rehearse in your mind how you would flee in the event of an emergency. Should something occur, you will have already thought through the best way to respond and will be better mentally prepared to implement your plan.

Leave everything behind. Forget about your purse, briefcase, and coat. Your objective is to move as fast as possible and as soon as possible. Don't stop for anything, other than to assist others also attempting to flee, if you feel you are able to help. However, if there are others that for whatever reason choose not to run, but instead want to stay behind and hide, it is not your responsibility to stay behind as well. If you think you can do so successfully, running away is your wisest course of action.

When you do run remember that law enforcement will be responding and they won't know who the bad guy is, and they certainly won't know you. A standard law enforcement safety procedure when responding to such an incident is to treat everyone as if they are the bad guys. It is not unheard of that an attacker will discard their weapon and then try to flee the location with everyone else, seeking to blend into the crowd as just another one of the victims. This is one of the reasons that law enforcement will treat everyone as a potential threat until proven otherwise.

Therefore, make sure as you run out into the open that you put your empty hands in air to let the police know that you are unarmed and not a threat to officers. You may be detained, and perhaps even handcuffed, but remember this is a precaution for the safety of both law enforcement and yourself.

Once a person is handcuffed, they pose less of a danger to police, so there is less possibility the handcuffed person's actions can be interpreted as threatening; a threat would require some type of police response. If you are detained it will only be for a short period of time, so remain cooperative with the police and answer their questions, helping them establish where the real threat exists.

Barring being able to run, the next option is to hide. But hiding will involve more than just ducking behind a desk. Find an office or room where you can lock the door. Even after locking the door, if you can, further barricade the entrance by pushing objects in front of it such as filing cabinets or furniture. This will make it more difficult for the attacker to enter the room should they try to do so. Once secured inside the room, look around at your options and determine if there are alternative avenues of escape should it become necessary. Is there another door leading to a separate area of the building, or can you easily break a window and jump to safety?

Close all blinds and stay away from any windows to prevent the shooter from seeing you. Also, you should turn off the lights along with anything else in the room that might make noise or attract the attention of the attacker. That includes making sure your cell phones are silenced so that the ringing does not give your location away.

Remain silent. Even if the attacker continues to attempt to open the door after finding that it is locked, as long as you are quiet the shooter will not know for certain if someone is inside the room. With luck the attacker will hopefully move along after a few unsuccessful attempts to gain entry.

Finally, look for whatever is in the room that you can use as a weapon. If the attacker is persistent in getting into the room, and there are no other avenues of escape, then you must be prepared to confront the danger if the shooter forces his or her way in.

Be prepared to surprise the attacker by staying close to the wall next to the door; as soon as the shooter comes in, strike first. You already know the attacker's purpose for being there is to kill, so there is no reason to wait and give the shooter any extra advantage in time. Strike first, surprising the shooter, and don't stop until you are certain the attacker has been sufficiently subdued in order for you to safely get away.

Assuming that you have been able to safely remain hidden, even if you are certain the danger has passed and that the attacker has moved on, do not leave the safety of where you have locked yourself in. Instead, try to quietly signal for help. You can post a message in the window letting rescuers know where you are, or use a phone to quietly call 9-1-1. You should remain in place until law enforcement has either indicated it is safe to exit, or the police have come to where you are hidden to retrieve you and bring you to safety.

Again, even if you have contacted the police, they won't immediately know if you are a threat. For all the police know you could be the attacker attempting to lure them by pretending to be a victim. Show your empty hands to the police, raising them above your head, and follow any instructions you are given.

Lastly, if running or hiding are not options, then the only choice left is to fight. But let me be clear: your objective is not to take on and defeat the attacker. Your goal is only to cause enough of a problem to disrupt or incapacitate the attacker to give you sufficient time to get away. This can be as little as pushing the shooter from behind to knock him or her to floor. In the time it takes for the shooter to get up and ready his weapon, you can be long gone.

In a fight with an attacker there are no rules. Use anything at your disposal. Throw chairs and furniture, hit them over the head with a metal fire extinguisher or discharge the CO_2 into their face. Likewise, get everyone who may be with you involved. There is strength in numbers, and if you are gathered together as a group then encourage everyone to fight by throwing whatever they can at the attacker. If you're in a restaurant, saltshakers, napkin holders, plates, food, beverages, a briefcase or purse, or a flowerpot can be your "weapons" to fight back against the active shooter.

The attacker can only focus on one or two persons at a time, and the more people that are fighting the attacker, the more likely it is they will be overpowered or even possibly retreat from the resistance. During the shooting incident that involved Congresswoman Gabriel Giffords and others in Tucson, Arizona, it is well documented that as the shooter attempted to reload his weapon several unarmed bystanders overpowered him and held him to the ground until police arrived, preventing further carnage.

If you are with other persons during an active shooting situation, and time allows, discuss a plan of what you are going to do should you have to fight the attacker. The attacker will not be expecting you to fight back. The element of surprise and the use of violent opposition will give you and any others an advantage to escape.

Regardless of how you escape from the active shooter, whether running, hiding, or fighting, a first responder will be the first person you will likely encounter. While remembering that you want to make sure the police recognize you as a victim and not a possible threat by holding your hands in the air above your head, you also want to be prepared to give the police as much information as you can.

Try to remember everything you can about the attacker so you can describe the shooter to police. If the shooter is someone with whom you are familiar, such as a coworker, obviously this will be easier. However, if the attacker is a stranger, do your best to remember the basics. Male or female, race, what he or she was wearing, etc.

Some of the key things to tell law enforcement is the last known location of the shooter, how many shooters you believe are involved, and if the attacker is still shooting. Law enforcement is trained to immediately confront these threats, often disregarding their own personal safety in an effort to save lives.

If you know of persons who were shot or injured that are still inside the building, tell the police this as well. Be sure to include where these victims can be found and the type of injuries they might have. A critical injury will require an immediate law enforcement extraction, but a lesser wound, such as a gunshot to the hand, can be delayed in the interest of first retrieving a more critically injured victim.

The type of weapon that the active shooter is using is very important as well, so that law enforcement is properly prepared to defend themselves. Some weapons will have more penetrating power than others, in some cases conceivably rendering standard police ballistic vests useless. If the active shooter is heavily armed with a long gun the police will undoubtedly require more protection like ballistic shields. However, don't be surprised if this information does not deter officers without this equipment from entering the scene anyway to confront the attacker. This speaks to the dedication and character of law enforcement that is so common. But telling law enforcement officials the type of weapon the active shooter is using helps the police know what they are up against.

Also it's just as important to let the police know how many weapons you think the shooter has, especially if you think the attacker may have come armed with explosives, such as grenades or pipe bombs. Every bit of information you provide can help keep responders a bit safer as they are doing their job of trying to rescue others and bring the attack to an end.

Finally, if you managed to escape before police have arrived, immediately call 9-1-1 and provide this same information to the police dispatcher so that the responding officers know everything possible before they arrive on the scene to take on the threat. The information you provide might be critical in saving lives.

I-TIP: They come to kill us. We must spot them, escape, hide, call 9-1-1, and possibly fight back.

CHAPTER TWELVE

CONTACTING THE AUTHORITIES

Terrorists don't want us to spot their actions or contact law enforcement. We must spot terror indicators and contact the authorities.

"Every day, first responders put their own lives on the line to ensure our safety. The least we can do is make sure they have the tools to protect and serve their communities."

—*Joe Lieberman**

As former Connecticut Senator and Vice Presidential nominee Joe Lieberman proclaims so well in the quotation above, our first responders must have the tools they need. And in today's increased-terror-threat world, our eyes and ears are big parts of the toolkit that first responders use to keep our communities, our homes, workplaces, and our loved ones safe.

Whether it is the FBI and other federal agencies, or the state and local police who protect us, our ability to spot and report potential threats to law enforcement authorities is essential. This chapter explains how and to whom you can report terror indicators before it's too late.

(See the "Stop Terror Resources" section in the Appendix section for information, forms, and links to helpful government websites, or visit howtospot.com/resources.)

---

*Joe Lieberman was a US Senator (Connecticut) and Vice Presidential Nominee.

Terrorists need money and they have many things to do before carrying out their acts of injury and death. As has been discussed there are supplies to gather and perhaps surveillance to conduct. A terrorist might try to impersonate someone like a delivery person or first responder as a cover story to facilitate the gathering of information, like what was done in the planned Fort Dix attack.

They might have been inspired to engage in terrorism through social media, and continue to use the Internet to obtaining terrorist training as well as inspire others to commit such acts, as the San Bernardino terrorist couple had been so engaged.

Terrorists might try to carry out their crimes through the use of a backpack to conceal a weapon, like in the Boston Marathon bombings. Clothing might be another terror tool in their arsenal to conceal or hide weapons they carry, or maybe it will be inside the vehicle they are driving or park, like the car bomb attempt in Times Square.

If they do attack, hopefully the terrorists will be unsuccessful, but if not immediately caught, perhaps they will leave behind their telltale signs of sabotage. In any event, my law enforcement experience tells me that after all of their necessary preparation efforts the terrorist may very well conduct a test run to practice the intended plan of death and destruction.

All of the indicators I summarized above and delivered throughout this book seek to bring to your attention that there is a giant opportunity for alert eyes and vigilant awareness to spot terror and report it. You've read my constant refrain to report suspicious things to police. Now here's your guide to help report what you have observed.

When in doubt call your local police by dialing 9-1-1. Even if the situation is not very dramatic, but you think there might be an imminent danger, let caution lead your decisions and report to law enforcement what you see and hear. Police agencies know the questions to ask to help you provide the best and most necessary information so that they can properly assess the situation.

If the situation is not an actual emergency, just something that makes you suspicious, call the police using the department's non-emergency number. These calls are answered and recorded twenty-four hours a day just like 9-1-1 calls, but if your call isn't a true emergency then you won't have to be concerned with unnecessarily tying up the emergency system. Regardless, your local law enforcement can still assess and respond based upon the information you have provided. If need be, the police can then obtain additional support, such as involving other federal or state agencies.

These days it seems that few people even know the phone numbers to their close friends or family because of advanced phone technology. Every phone number we use is now stored in our phones, so there is little need for us to memorize them.

The odds of knowing your local police phone number is minimal at best. You may be able to do a quick online search with your computer or phone, but if things are happening rapidly, taking the time to conduct a search for the number to call might waste crucial minutes. Instead, as I recommended in the last chapter about having an emergency action plan (see plan resources in the "Stop Terror Resources" section in the Appendix), it is always best to be prepared.

Take a few moments and look up the police non-emergency phone number (while you are at it, look up the numbers for fire, ambulance, and poison control as well). Save them in your contacts and e-mail them to your family and friends. If you know those who don't use today's technology, provide them a copy so that they have it written down.

Let's not forget that technology can fail. Print several copies of your emergency planning documents and contact information, and have them somewhere safe and easily retrievable when they are needed.

Law enforcement is trained to help, so if and when you call they will know what to do. You will probably be asked for further details, so when calling 9-1-1 or the non-emergency line, be prepared to provide enough basic information in order for a police operator to be able to evaluate your call and dispatch the proper response. Here are some of the basics you will want to tell the police operator:

- Provide a brief description of the activity about which you are concerned.

- Give the date, time, and location of the activity in question.

- Provide information regarding any physical identifiers of the subjects you observed, to include the race, sex, approximate height, weight, age, and clothing worn, etc.

- Provide a description of any relevant vehicles. The license plate is best, but whether you are able to obtain the license plate information or not, be sure to note the make, model, and color, and whether the vehicle has two or four doors.

- Only if it is completely safe for you take a picture with your phone, do so; it can prove to be much more accurate than our perception in the moment, in addition to having evidentiary value later on.

- If the people involved in the activity you observed have left the area, try to provide any details regarding where they may have gone and their direction of travel.

- Finally, provide your name and the phone number at which you can be reached should the police have any additional questions later on.

It may be of comfort to some reading this book that you can decline to give your personal information and simply explain that you prefer to remain anonymous. Authorities won't be mad at you or give you a hard time to remain unnamed or anonymous. The important thing is that you make the call.

In the aftermath of the 2015 San Bernardino attack, neighbors discussed their earlier suspicions that some things just weren't right at the terror subjects' residence. Unfortunately, none of them contacted law enforcement. It is understandable that some are hesitant to call the police based upon just a suspicion, especially if after the police become involved it turns out to be nothing. However, be assured that regardless of however the matter turns out, no one would ever find out that you are the person who contacted law enforcement.

Police are experienced in taking reports and maintaining the privacy of how the information was obtained. If your call to police turns out to be nothing, no one will ever know the difference. If it turns out to be something, you might just have saved lives.

In addition to calling the police, many local and federal agencies now have the means of making a report online. You can send an e-mail or click a link that asks you to fill in the blanks for information. An Internet search of the law enforcement agency's name and "how to make a report" should quickly assist you in finding what you need. Bookmark the link and have it ready and available for when you need it.

If the activity you have observed is an indicator of a possible terrorist act, call the FBI. The FBI has fifty-six field offices nationwide, in addition to approximately four hundred smaller satellite offices that are known as Resident Agencies. Additionally, the FBI now has overseas "Legat" offices in more than sixty-two countries around the world, working with international law enforcement agencies to solve crimes and prevent terrorism that affects us here in the United States.

For your convenience I have included a list of the fifty-six FBI field offices, including addresses and telephone numbers (see the "Stop Terror Resources" guide for the FBI offices list in the Appendix or visit howtospot.com/resources). Additionally, here are a couple of the links that might be helpful if you spot something that you think should be reported:

https://tips.fbi.gov

This link is for reporting any information regarding a possible crime or terrorist activity and will be forwarded to the appropriate FBI office for a follow-up investigation.

https://www.fbi.gov/contact-us/field/field-offices

This link provides the list of all fifty-six field offices' addresses and telephone information; this list is also in the Appendix.

https://www.fbi.gov/contact-us/legat/legal_offices

This link provides a list of all of the FBI overseas Legat office addresses and telephone information, should you be traveling abroad. Otherwise, even if you are aware of something occurring overseas, if you are within the United States call your local FBI office.

https://www.infragard.org

If you own a business, especially one that plays any role whatsoever in supporting an aspect of our critical infrastructure (computers, finance, retail business, etc.) look into becoming a member of InfraGard.

InfraGard is a public/private alliance established by the FBI that brings these businesses together to share information with one another regarding different threats that have been encountered in the business world. Additionally, the FBI provides intelligence briefings to the

InfraGard members, supplying you information to protect yourselves against threats that is not otherwise available to the average person. Your membership in InfraGard will give you a definite advantage in the private sector to ensure your business's safety and security.

Finally, in addition to links to websites, ongoing advances in technology will make future information reporting even easier. There are now downloadable applications that utilize the benefits of your smart phone when reporting possible indicators.

One such company, Close Watch Technologies, Inc., has developed a smart phone app that enables users to directly submit crime and terrorism tips, along with text, images, and videos pertaining to any type of incident. The app automatically forwards the information to the appropriate law enforcement agency, which helps facilitate a quicker resolution. To obtain the app you can visit the Close Watch Technologies website, http://www.closewatchtechnologies.com, or download the app from iTunes by searching "iWatch."

It is just a matter of time before reporting information via your smart phone app will be the norm, sharing with the authorities critical information in a manner that is faster and more complete, thereby making us all safer.

Your ability to spot and identify terror indicators requires prompt and detailed reporting of anything suspicious to the local police or FBI. Whether you call, e-mail, text, clink on a website link, or use the latest smart phone application, your involvement can help prevent a future violent terrorist attack. Once again, if you see something, let law enforcement know.

I-TIP: Terrorists don't want us to spot their actions or contact law enforcement. We must spot terror indicators and contact the authorities.

STOP TERROR RESOURCES

1. FBI OFFICES BY STATE

A

Alabama

FBI Birmingham
1000 18th Street North
Birmingham, AL 35203
birmingham.fbi.gov
(205) 326-6166

FBI Mobile
200 N. Royal Street
Mobile, AL 36602
mobile.fbi.gov
(251) 438-3674

Alaska

FBI Anchorage
101 East Sixth Avenue
Anchorage, AK 99501-2524
anchorage.fbi.gov
(907) 276-4441

Arizona

FBI Phoenix
21711 N. 7th Street
Phoenix, AZ 85024-5118
phoenix.fbi.gov
(623) 466-1999

Arkansas

FBI Little Rock
#24 Shackleford West Boulevard
Little Rock, AR 72211-3755
littlerock.fbi.gov
(501) 221-9100

C

California

FBI Los Angeles
Suite 1700, FOB
11000 Wilshire Boulevard
Los Angeles, CA 90024-3672
losangeles.fbi.gov
(310) 477-6565

FBI Sacramento
4500 Orange Grove Avenue
Sacramento, CA 95841-4205
sacramento.fbi.gov
(916) 481-9110

FBI San Diego
10385 Vista Sorrento Parkway
San Diego, CA 92121
sandiego.fbi.gov
(858) 320-1800

FBI San Francisco
450 Golden Gate Avenue, 13th
    Floor
San Francisco, CA 94102-9523
sanfrancisco.fbi.gov
(415) 553-7400

Colorado

FBI Denver
8000 East 36th Avenue
Denver, CO 80238
denver.fbi.gov
(303) 629-7171

Connecticut

FBI New Haven
600 State Street
New Haven, CT 06511-6505
newhaven.fbi.gov
(203) 777-6311

D

District of Columbia

FBI Washington
Washington Metropolitan
    Field Office
601 4th Street, N.W.
Washington, D.C. 20535-0002
washingtondc.fbi.gov
(202) 278-2000
For FBI Headquarters in
    Washington, D.C., see the
    "Contact Us" page

F

Florida

FBI Jacksonville
6061 Gate Parkway
Jacksonville, FL 32256
jacksonville.fbi.gov
(904) 248-7000

FBI Miami
2030 SW 145th Avenue
Miramar, FL 33027
miami.fbi.gov
(754) 703-2000

FBI Tampa
5525 West Gray Street
Tampa, FL 33609
tampa.fbi.gov
(813) 253-1000

G

Georgia

FBI Atlanta
Suite 400
2635 Century Parkway,
  Northeast
Atlanta, GA 30345-3112
atlanta.fbi.gov
(404) 679-9000

H

Hawaii

FBI Honolulu
91-1300 Enterprise Street
Kapolei, HI 96707
honolulu.fbi.gov
(808) 566-4300

I

Illinois

FBI Chicago
2111 West Roosevelt Road
  Chicago, IL 60608-1128
chicago.fbi.gov
(312) 421-6700

FBI Springfield
900 East Linton Avenue
Springfield, IL 62703
springfield.fbi.gov
(217) 522-9675

Indiana

FBI Indianapolis
8825 Nelson B Klein Pkwy
Indianapolis, IN 46250
indianapolis.fbi.gov
(317) 595-4000

K

Kentucky

FBI Louisville
12401 Sycamore Station Place
Louisville, KY
40299-6198
louisville.fbi.gov
(502) 263-6000

L

Louisiana

FBI New Orleans
2901 Leon C. Simon Dr.
New Orleans, LA 70126
neworleans.fbi.gov
(504) 816-3000

M

Maryland

FBI Baltimore
2600 Lord Baltimore Drive
Baltimore, MD 21244
baltimore.fbi.gov
(410) 265-8080

Massachusetts

FBI Boston
Suite 600
One Center Plaza
Boston, MA 02108
boston.fbi.gov
(617) 742-5533

Michigan

FBI Detroit
26th Floor, P. V. McNamara FOB
477 Michigan Avenue
Detroit, MI 48226
detroit.fbi.gov
(313) 965-2323

Minnesota

FBI Minneapolis
1501 Freeway Boulevard
Brooklyn Center, MN 55430
minneapolis.fbi.gov
(763) 569-8000

Mississippi

FBI Jackson
1220 Echelon Parkway
Jackson, MS 39213
jackson.fbi.gov
(601) 948-5000

Missouri

FBI Kansas City
1300 Summit
Kansas City, MO 64105-1362
kansascity.fbi.gov
(816) 512-8200

FBI St. Louis
2222 Market Street
St. Louis, MO 63103-2516
stlouis.fbi.gov
(314) 231-4324

N

Nebraska

FBI Omaha
4411 South 121st Court
Omaha, NE 68137-2112
omaha.fbi.gov
(402) 493-8688

Nevada

FBI Las Vegas
John Lawrence Bailey Building
1787 West Lake Mead Boulevard
Las Vegas, NV 89106-2135
lasvegas.fbi.gov
(702) 385-1281

New Jersey

FBI Newark
11 Centre Place
Newark, NJ 07102-9889
newark.fbi.gov
(973) 792-3000

New Mexico

FBI Albuquerque
4200 Luecking Park Ave. NE
Albuquerque, NM 87107
albuquerque.fbi.gov
(505) 889-1300

New York

FBI Albany
200 McCarty Avenue
Albany, NY 12209
albany.fbi.gov
(518) 465-7551

FBI Buffalo
One FBI Plaza
Buffalo, NY 14202-2698
buffalo.fbi.gov
(716) 856-7800

FBI New York
26 Federal Plaza, 23rd Floor
New York, NY 10278-0004
newyork.fbi.gov
(212) 384-1000

North Carolina

FBI Charlotte
7915 Microsoft Way
Charlotte, NC 28273
charlotte.fbi.gov
(704) 672-6100

O

Ohio

FBI Cincinnati
2012 Ronald Reagan Drive
Cincinnati, OH 45236
cincinnati.fbi.gov
(513) 421-4310

FBI Cleveland
Federal Office Building
1501 Lakeside Avenue
Cleveland, OH 44114
cleveland.fbi.gov
(216) 522-1400

Oklahoma

FBI Oklahoma City
3301 West Memorial Drive
Oklahoma City, OK 73134
oklahomacity.fbi.gov
(405) 290-7770

Oregon

FBI Portland
9109 NE Cascades Parkway
Portland, OR 97220
portland.fbi.gov
(503) 224-4181

P

Pennsylvania

FBI Philadelphia
8th Floor
William J. Green Jr. FOB
600 Arch Street
Philadelphia, PA 19106
philadelphia.fbi.gov
(215) 418-4000

FBI Pittsburgh
3311 East Carson St.
Pittsburgh, PA 15203
pittsburgh.fbi.gov
(412) 432-4000

Puerto Rico

FBI San Juan
Room 526, US Federal Bldg.
150 Carlos Chardon Avenue
  Hato Rey
San Juan, PR 00918-1716
sanjuan.fbi.gov
(787) 754-6000

S

South Carolina

FBI Columbia
151 Westpark Blvd
Columbia, SC 29210-3857
columbia.fbi.gov
(803) 551-4200

T

Tennessee

FBI Knoxville
1501 Dowell Springs Boulevard
Knoxville, TN 37909
knoxville.fbi.gov
(865) 544-0751

FBI Memphis
Suite 3000, Eagle Crest Bldg.
225 North Humphreys Blvd.
Memphis, TN 38120-2107
memphis.fbi.gov
(901) 747-4300

Texas

FBI Dallas
One Justice Way
Dallas, Texas 75220
dallas.fbi.gov
(972) 559-5000

FBI El Paso
660 S. Mesa Hills Drive
El Paso, Texas 79912-5533
elpaso.fbi.gov
(915) 832-5000

FBI Houston
1 Justice Park Drive
Houston, TX 77092
houston.fbi.gov
(713) 693-5000

FBI San Antonio
5740 University Heights
Boulevard
San Antonio, TX 78249
sanantonio.fbi.gov
(210) 225-6741

U

Utah

FBI Salt Lake City
5425 West Amelia Earhart Drive
Salt Lake City, UT 84116
saltlakecity.fbi.gov
(801) 579-1400

V

Virginia

FBI Norfolk
509 Resource Row
Chesapeake, VA 23320
norfolk.fbi.gov
(757) 455-0100

FBI Richmond
1970 E. Parham Road
Richmond, VA 23228
richmond.fbi.gov
(804) 261-1044
For Northern Virginia, contact
the Washington Field Office.

W

Washington

FBI Seattle
1110 Third Avenue
Seattle, WA 98101-2904
seattle.fbi.gov
(206) 622-0460

Wisconsin

FBI Milwaukee
Suite 600
330 East Kilbourn Avenue
Milwaukee, WI 53202-6627
milwaukee.fbi.gov
(414) 276-4684

STOP TERROR RESOURCES

2. SAFETY TOOLS & RESOURCES

In this terror-threatened world, it is critically important to the safety of you and your loved ones to be prepared with as much knowledge as possible, and to know where to turn for assistance.

To help you, the publisher has created a resource guide on the SafeLife Publishing website. It offers expanded knowledge and more in depth guidance on:

1. *Learn how to create a Household Disaster Plan*

2. *Find out how to help and protect yourself, co-workers and loved ones when faced with terror and other disasters*

3. *Get access to mobile apps to get terror and disaster information and to receive alerts, get safety reminders, locate shelters, upload and share photos to help first responders*

4. *Review the findings of the The 9/11 Commission Report*

5. *See how terrorists use and move money around*

6. *Learn how terrorists use impersonation of first responders and how to spot it*

7. *Find out about how to protect yourself from Terrorist Cyber Threats*

8. *Be empowered to spot Suspicious Terror Activity and Indicators*

9. *Learn the best ways to spot and report Terrorists' Suspicious Activity*

Go to: safelifepublishing.com Twitter: @forasaferlife
Facebook: SafeLife Publishing
YouTube: SafeLife Publishing
http://lnked.in/safelifepublishing

GLOSSARY TERMS

active shooter—an individual actively engaged in killing or attempting to kill people, generally choosing to do so in populated areas.

al-Qaeda—a militant Sunni Islamist global organization founded in 1988 by Osama bin Laden, Abdullah Azzam, and several other Arab volunteers who fought against the Soviet invasion of Afghanistan in the 1980s.

ATF—a law enforcement agency charged with the investigation of the illegal use and trafficking of firearms, the illegal use and storage of explosives, acts of arson and bombings, acts of terrorism, and the illegal diversion of alcohol and tobacco products.

car bomb—commonly used as a weapon of assassination, terrorism or guerrilla warfare, to kill the occupants of the vehicle, people near the blast site, or to damage buildings or other property.

catfishing—someone who pretends to be someone they're not through the use of social media to create false identities, particularly to pursue deceptive online romances.

China syndrome—a hypothetical nuclear reactor accident in which the fuel would melt through the floor of the containment structure and burrow into the earth, "all the way to China."

cloned vehicles—cars and trucks that have been disguised to look like police, fire, or other official vehicles.

FBI—The Federal Bureau of Investigation, which serves as the nation's premiere federal law enforcement agency.

"Going Dark"—Law enforcement reference to the inability to monitor communications due to encryption by sophisticated technologies, ever lawfully authorized to conduct such monitoring.

high-value targets—parts of an infrastructure that are targeted by terrorist organizations, such as power transmission lines, power substations, communications facilities, natural gas supplies, and generating facilities.

I-TIP—The Iannarelli Terrorist Indicator Profile. Simple suggestions to guide you on how to spot terrorist indicators and help law enforcement by reporting what you see.

impersonation—the art and science of pretending to be someone else and fooling others.

improvised explosive device (IED)— a bomb constructed and deployed in ways other than in conventional military action. It may be constructed of conventional military explosives, such as an artillery round, attached to a detonating mechanism.

ISIS—is a Salafi jihadist militant group that follows an Islamic fundamentalist, Wahhabi doctrine of Sunni Islam.

jihad—an Islamic term referring to the religious duty of Muslims to maintain the religion.

"lone wolf"—an extremist or terrorist not acting on the direction of another person but, rather, acting on his or her own, but may have been influenced by the teachings of others.

material support—applies primarily to groups designated as terrorists by the US Department of State. The four types of support described are "training," "expert advice or assistance," "service," and "personnel."

profiling—the recording and analysis of a person's psychological and behavioral characteristics, so as to assess or predict their capabilities in a certain sphere or to assist in identifying a particular subgroup of people.

sabotage—a deliberate action aimed at weakening a polity or corporation through subversion, obstruction, disruption or destruction.

surveillance—the attentive observation of a person or place for the purpose of obtaining information. Often a terrorist will gather information about a potential target during the planning stages of an attack in an effort to identify potential security weaknesses that might be targeted.

terrorism—the use of violence, or threatened use of violence, in order to achieve a political, religious, or ideological aim.

terrorist—a person who uses terrorism in the pursuit of political aims.

test runs—a terrorist tactic to ensure the success of achieving death and destruction.

vandalism—action involving deliberate destruction of or damage to public or private property.

ABOUT THE AUTHOR

John G. Iannarelli retired from the FBI after more than twenty years of service, during time which he participated in the investigations of the Oklahoma City Bombing, the 9/11 terrorists attacks, and the Congresswoman Gabriel Giffords shooting, among many others significant events.

During his career John served in the Detroit and San Diego Divisions before being transferred to FBI Headquarters in Washington, DC, where he served as the Bureau's national spokesperson. He was later assigned to the FBI's Cyber Division before being made a supervisor in the Phoenix Division. He was subsequently promoted to become the Assistant Special Agent in Charge of the office: the FBI's number two position for entire state of Arizona.

John has been awarded an honorary doctorate degree of computer science for his contributions to the field of cyber investigations, and is a recipient of the FBI's Directors Award for Distinguished Service. He is also an attorney and a former San Diego police officer.

John is currently president of the JGI Consulting Group, which provides services to clients in both the private and government sectors. He is a speaker who is in high demand, having presented worldwide to hundreds of audiences for Fortune 500 companies, the United Nations, and even at the Vatican.

You can learn more about John, along with his speaking and consulting services, by visiting his website at JohnIannarelli.com. You can also follow him on Twitter @JohngIannarelli.

ALSO BY JOHN G. IANNARELLI

Information Governance and Security: Protecting and Managing Your Company's Proprietary Information

Information Governance and Security shows managers in any size organization how to create and implement the policies, procedures and training necessary to keep their organizations most important asset-its proprietary information-safe from cyber and physical compromise.

Many intrusions can be prevented if appropriate precautions are taken, and this book establishes the enterprise-level systems and disciplines necessary for managing all the information generated by an organization. In addition, the book encompasses the human element by considering proprietary information lost, damaged, or destroyed through negligence. By implementing the policies and procedures outlined in Information Governance and Security, organizations can proactively protect their reputation against the threats that most managers have never even considered.

ISBN: 978-0-12-800247-6

W.T.F.: Why Teens Fail—What To Fix

We've all seen some poor adolescent spiral out of control and hoped that it would never be our kid making those kinds of mistakes. Why do some teens self-destruct? Can we communicate a little differently? Can we teach or encourage a little more? When do we let them make mistakes and face the consequences and when do we jump in to their rescue?

This book contains true stories of parents and teens, written by professionals who interact with teens in a variety of ways. Cops, teachers, administrators and counselors all provide valuable insight to parents about how to help your teens avoid the serious pitfalls of adolescence and capitalize on their mistakes for future success. WTF? Failure is not an option!

ISBN 061570493X
ISBN-13: 978-0615704937

The Eighty Thieves: American P.O.W.s in Japan

The Eighty Thieves story tells of the short battle for Guam against overwhelming odds. Captured and taken to Japan, the prisoners were forced to work as slaves at the Nippon Sietesu steel mills (Nippon Iron and Steel, as NKK was known as before the war).

Iannarelli gives a detailed and stirring account of bravery by these prisoners as they endured endless days of starvation, savagery, and brutality at the hands of the Japanese guards. Iannarelli's father was one of these prisoners and he had the advantage of speaking Japanese, thereby being able to prevent much of the savagery against fellow inmates by interpreting Japanese commands. Like the 80 fellow POWs from Guam, Iannarelli's father learned to steal food and supplies in order to live. Being caught meant a savage beating with baseball bats and mass punishments of the entire camp.

Reviewed as one of the singular best books written about the Hirohata POW camp. Worth acquiring for the serious student of World War II history.

ISBN-10: 0963038400

For more information and links to purchase these books, please visit johniannarelli.com

INDEX

CL●SEWATCH
TECHNOLOGIES, INC.

More information in Chapter 12 on page 87

Made in the USA
Lexington, KY
07 July 2016